YOUR PERSONAL ASTROLOGY PLANNER

LIBRA

2008

YOUR PERSONAL ASTROLOGY PLANNER

LIBRA 2008

RICK LEVINE & **JEFF** JAWER

STERLING

New York / London
www.sterlingpublishing.com

Library of Congress Cataloging-in-Publication Data Available

2 4 6 8 10 9 7 5 3 1

Published by Sterling Publishing Co., Inc.
387 Park Avenue South, New York, NY 10016

Distributed in Canada by Sterling Publishing
c/o Canadian Manda Group, 165 Dufferin Street
Toronto, Ontario, Canada M6K 3H6
Distributed in the United Kingdom by GMC Distribution Services
Castle Place, 166 High Street, Lewes, East Sussex, England BN7 1XU
Distributed in Australia by Capricorn Link (Australia) Pty. Ltd.
P.O. Box 704, Windsor, NSW 2756, Australia

Original book design: 3+Co., New York

Manufactured in the United States of America

Sterling ISBN-13: 978-1-4027-4848-6
ISBN-10: 1-4027-4848-5

TABLE OF CONTENTS

THE PURPOSE OF THIS BOOK

The more you learn about yourself, the better able you are to wisely use the energies in your life. For more than 3,000 years, astrology has been the sharpest tool in the box for describing the human condition. Used by virtually every culture on the planet, astrology continues to serve as a link between individual lives and planetary cycles. We gain valuable insights into personal issues with a birth chart, and can plot the patterns of the year ahead in meaningful ways for individuals as well as groups. You share your sun sign with eight percent of humanity. Clearly, you're not all going to have the same day, even if the basic astrological cycles are the same. Your individual circumstances, the specific factors of your entire birth chart, and your own free will help you write your unique story.

The purpose of this book is to describe the energies of the Sun, Moon, and planets for the year ahead and help you create your future, rather than being a victim of it. We aim to facilitate your journey by showing you the turns ahead in the road of life and hopefully the best ways to navigate them.

YOU ARE THE STAR OF YOUR LIFE

It is not our goal to simply predict events. Rather, we are reporting the planetary energies—the cosmic weather in which you are living—so that you understand these conditions and know how to use them most effectively.

The power, though, isn't in the stars, but in your mind, your heart, and the choices that you make every day. Regardless of how strongly you are buffeted by the winds of change or bored by stagnation, you have many ways to view any situation. Learning about the energies of the Sun, Moon, and planets will both sharpen and widen your perspective, thereby giving you additional choices.

The language of astrology is a gift of awareness, not a rigid set of rules. It works best when blended with common sense, intuition, and self-trust. This is your life, and no one knows how to live it as well as you. Take what you need from this book and leave the rest. Although the planets set the stage for the year ahead, you're the writer, director, and star of your life and you can play the part in whatever way you choose. *Your Personal Astrology Planner* uses information about your sun sign to give you a better understanding of how the planetary waves will wash upon your shore. We each navigate our lives through time, and each moment has unique qualities. Astrology gives us the ability to describe the constantly changing timescape. For example, if you know the trajectory and the speed of an approaching storm, you can choose to delay a leisurely afternoon sail on the bay, thus avoiding an unpleasant situation.

By reading this book, you can improve your ability to align with the cosmic weather, the larger patterns that affect you day to day. You can become more effective by aligning with the cosmos and cocreating the year ahead with a better understanding of the energies around you.

Astrology doesn't provide quick fixes to life's complex issues. It doesn't offer neatly packed black-and-white answers in a world filled with an infinite variety of shapes and colors. It can, however, give you a much clearer picture of the invisible forces influencing your life.

ENERGY & EVENTS

Two sailboats can face the same gale yet travel in opposite directions as a result of how the sails are positioned. Similarly, how you respond to the energy of a particular set of circumstances may be more responsible for your fate than the given situation itself. We delineate the energetic winds for your year ahead, but your attitude shapes the unfolding events, and your responses alter your destiny.

This book emphasizes the positive, not because all is good, but because astrology shows us ways to transform even the power of a storm into beneficial results. Empowerment comes from learning to see the invisible energy patterns that impact the visible landscape as you fill in the details of your story every day on this spinning planet, orbited by the Moon, lit by the Sun, and colored by the nuances of the planets.

You are a unique point in an infinite galaxy of unlimited possibilities, and the choices that you make have consequences. So use this book in a most magical way to consciously improve your life.

MOON CHARTS

2008 NEW MOONS

Each New Moon marks the beginning of a cycle. In general, this is the best time to plant seeds for future growth. Use the days preceeding the New Moon to finish old business prior to starting what comes next. The focused mind can be quite sharp during this phase. Harness the potential of the New Moon by stating your intentions—out loud or in writing—for the weeks ahead. Hold these goals in your mind; help them grow to fruition through conscious actions as the Moon gains light during the following two weeks. In the chart below, the dates and times refer to when the Moon and Sun align in each zodiac sign (see p16), initiating a new lunar cycle.

DATE	TIME	SIGN
January 8	6:37 AM EST	Capricorn
February 6	10:43 PM EST	Aquarius **(ECLIPSE)**
March 7	12:13 PM EST	Pisces
April 5	11:54 PM EDT	Aries
May 5	8:18 AM EDT	Taurus
June 3	3:22 PM EDT	Gemini
July 2	10:19 PM EDT	Cancer
August 1	6:12 AM EDT	Leo **(ECLIPSE)**
August 30	3:58 PM EDT	Virgo
September 29	4:12 AM EDT	Libra
October 28	7:14 PM EDT	Scorpio
November 27	11:54 AM EST	Sagittarius
December 27	7:22 AM EST	Capricorn

2008 FULL MOONS

The Full Moon reflects the light of the Sun as subjective feelings reflect the objective events of the day. Dreams seem bigger; moods feel stronger. The emotional waters run with deeper currents. This is the phase of culmination, a turning point in the energetic cycle. Now it's time to listen to the inner voices. Rather than starting new projects, the two weeks after the Full Moon are when we complete what we can and slow our outward expressions in anticipation of the next New Moon. In this chart, the dates and times refer to when the moon is opposite the sun in each zodiac sign, marking the emotional peak of each lunar cycle.

DATE	TIME	SIGN
January 22	8:35 AM EST	Leo
February 20	10:31 PM EST	Virgo **(ECLIPSE)**
March 21	2:40 PM EDT	Libra
April 20	6:25 AM EDT	Scorpio
May 19	10:11 PM EDT	Scorpio
June 18	1:30 PM EDT	Sagittarius
July 18	3:58 AM EDT	Capricorn
August 16	5:16 PM EDT	Aquarius **(ECLIPSE)**
September 15	5:13 AM EDT	Pisces
October 14	4:01 PM EDT	Aries
November 13	1:16 AM EST	Taurus
December 12	11:37 AM EST	Gemini

ASTROLOGY, YOU & THE WORLD

WELCOME TO YOUR SUN SIGN

The Sun, Moon, and Earth and all the planets lie within a plane called the **ecliptic** and move through a narrow band of stars made up by 12 constellations called the **zodiac**. The Earth revolves around the Sun once a year, but from our point of view, it appears that the Sun moves through each sign of the zodiac for one month. There are 12 months and astrologically there are 12 signs. The astrological months, however, do not match our calendar, and start between the 19th and 23rd of each month. Everyone is born to an astrological month, like being born in a room with a particular perspective of the world. Knowing your sun sign provides useful information about your personality and your future, but for a more detailed astrological analysis, a full birth chart calculation based on your precise date, time, and place of birth is necessary. Get your complete birth chart online at:

http://www.tarot.com/astrology/astroprofile

This book is about your zodiac sign. Your Sun in the air sign of diplomatic Libra is highly sensitive to balance and harmony in relationships, which is why you're so concerned with fairness and maintaining the peace. Trying to keep other people happy is one of your gifts, even though sometimes you sacrifice too much of your own needs to make this happen. You are in your element when you connect with gracious people in attractive surroundings.

THE PLANETS

We refer to the Sun and Moon as planets. Don't worry; we do know about modern astronomy. Although the Sun is really a star and the Moon is a satellite, they are called planets for astrological purposes. The astrological planets are the Sun, the Moon, Mercury, Venus, Mars, Jupiter, Saturn, Chiron, Uranus, Neptune, and Pluto.

Your sun sign is the most obvious astrological placement, for the Sun returns to the same sign every year. But at the same time, the Moon is orbiting the Earth, changing signs every two and a third days. Mercury, Venus, and Mars each move through a sign in a few weeks to a few months.

Jupiter spends a whole year in a sign—and Pluto visits a sign for up to 30 years! The ever-changing positions of the planets alter the energetic terrain through which we travel. The planets are symbols; each has a particular range of meanings. For example, Venus is the goddess of love, but it really symbolizes beauty in a spectrum of experiences. Venus can represent romantic love, sensuality, the arts, or good food. It activates anything that we value, including personal possessions and even money. To our ancestors, the planets actually animated life on Earth. In this way of thinking, every beautiful flower contains the essence of Venus.

Each sign has a natural affinity to an individual planet, and as this planet moves through the sky, it sends messages of particular interest to people born under that sign. Venus, your key or ruling planet, is the goddess of love, beauty, pleasure and fine objects. Its movement shows where relationship and self-worth issues, the principles of attraction and desire, and money come into your life, as well as time when you're open to receiving gifts of all kinds. Planets can be described by many different words, for the mythology of each is a rich tapestry. In this book we use a variety of words when talking about each planet in order to convey the most applicable meaning. The table below describes a few keywords for each planet, including the Sun and Moon.

PLANET	SYMBOL	KEYWORDS
Sun	☉	Consciousness, Will, Vitality
Moon	☽	Subconscious, Emotions, Habits
Mercury	☿	Communication, Thoughts, Transportation
Venus	♀	Desire, Love, Money, Values
Mars	♂	Action, Physical Energy, Drive
Jupiter	♃	Expansion, Growth, Optimism
Saturn	♄	Contraction, Maturity, Responsibility
Chiron	⚷	Healing, Pain, Subversion
Uranus	♅	Awakening, Unpredictable, Inventive
Neptune	♆	Imagination, Spirituality, Confusion
Pluto	♇	Passion, Intensity, Regeneration

HOUSES

Just as planets move through the signs of the zodiac, they also move through the houses in an individual chart. The 12 houses correspond to the 12 signs, but are individualized, based upon your sign. In this book we use Solar Houses, which place your sun sign in your 1st House. Therefore, when a planet enters a new sign it also enters a new house. If you know your exact time of birth, the rising sign determines the 1st House. You can learn your rising sign by entering your birth date at:

http://www.tarot.com/astrology/astroprofile

HOUSE	SIGN	KEYWORDS
1st House	Aries	Self, Appearance, Personality
2nd House	Taurus	Possessions, Values, Self-Worth
3rd House	Gemini	Communication, Siblings, Short Trips
4th House	Cancer	Home, Family, Roots
5th House	Leo	Love, Romance, Children, Play
6th House	Virgo	Work, Health, Daily Routines
7th House	Libra	Marriage, Relationships, Business Partners
8th House	Scorpio	Intimacy, Transformation, Shared Resources
9th House	Sagittarius	Travel, Higher Education, Philosophy
10th House	Capricorn	Career, Community, Ambition
11th House	Aquarius	Groups and Friends, Associations, Social Ideals
12th House	Pisces	Imagination, Spirituality, Secret Activities

ASPECTS

As the planets move through the sky in their various cycles, they form ever-changing angles with one another. Certain angles create significant geometric shapes. So, when two planets are 90 degrees apart, they conform to a square; 60 degrees of separation conforms to a sextile, or six-pointed star. Planets create **aspects** when they're at these special angles. Aspects explain how the individual symbolism of pairs of planets combine into an energetic pattern.

ASPECT	DEGREES	KEYWORDS
Conjunction	0	Compression, Blending, Focus
Opposition	180	Tension, Awareness, Balance
Trine	120	Harmony, Free-Flowing, Ease
Square	90	Resistance, Stress, Dynamic Conflict
Quintile	72	Creativity, Metaphysical, Magic
Sextile	60	Support, Intelligent, Activating
Quincunx	150	Irritation, Annoyance, Adjustment

2008 GENERAL FORECAST:
THE INDIVIDUAL AND THE COLLECTIVE

Astrology works for individuals, groups, and even humanity as a whole. You will have your own story in 2008, but it will unfold among 6.7 billion other tales of human experience. We are each unique, yet our lives touch one another; our destinies are woven together by weather and war, by economy, science, politics, religion, and all the other threads of life on this planet. We make personal choices every day, yet there are great events beyond the control of any one individual. When the power goes out in a neighborhood, it affects everyone, yet individual astrology patterns will describe the personal response of each person.

We are living at a time when the tools of self-awareness fill bookshelves, Web sites, and broadcasts, and we benefit greatly from them. Yet despite all this wisdom, conflicts among groups cause enormous suffering. Understanding personal issues is a powerful means for increasing happiness, but knowledge of our collective issues is equally important for our well-being. This forecast of the major trends and planetary patterns for 2008 provides a framework for understanding the potentials and challenges we face together, so that we can advance with tolerance and respect as a community and fulfill our potentials as individuals.

The astrological events used for this forecast are the transits of major planets Jupiter and Saturn, the retrograde cycles of Mercury, and the eclipses of the Sun and the Moon.

A NOTE ABOUT THE DATES IN THIS BOOK

All events are based upon the Eastern Time Zone of the United States. Because of local time differences, an event occurring just minutes after midnight in the East will actually happen the prior day in the rest of the country. Although the key dates are the exact dates of any particular alignment, some of you are so ready for certain things to happen that you can react to a transit a day or two before it is exact. And sometimes you could be so entrenched in habits or unwilling to change that you may not notice the effects right away. Allow extra time around each key date to feel the impact of any event.

JUPITER IN CAPRICORN
MATERIALIZING SUCCESS
December 18, 2007–January 5, 2009

Optimistic Jupiter is ready to climb a mountain this year. Instead of simply heading off on an adventure, the planet of expansion's passage through industrious Capricorn is a time to set goals, plan a course of action, and reach the summit of success. Jolly Jupiter is usually happy exploring the world, seeking new experiences, and expanding the mind. But Saturn-ruled Capricorn puts the giant planet in a productive mood where the name of the game is getting results. Opportunities come for those who do their homework and demonstrate the patience and commitment to prove their worthiness. There's less room for sloppiness for those who want chance to turn in their favor. Good luck is earned only by solid effort this year.

Jupiter in Capricorn is a time to turn beliefs into reality. Idealistic philosophies lose their meaning unless practice brings them down to earth. The enormous planet loves the biggest ideas, but Capricorn's practicality will test them against the weight of experience. The dark side of Jupiter's presence here is materialism that values worldly achievement more than spiritual awakening. Instead of living up to standards that may be difficult to reach, it will be tempting to lower those standards or just do away with them entirely.

Hope for a balanced approach to ambition occurs with positive trines between Jupiter and Saturn in January, September, and November. These healthy alignments between the planets of expansion and contraction bring the wisdom of self-restraint and a willingness to earn one's rewards honestly. Those who play by the rules should get what they deserve, while those who cut corners are likely to slide right off the track and slip farther from their aspirations. The Jupiter-Saturn trine in earth signs adds conscientiousness and a capacity to put in the time necessary to attain one's goals.

Positive 60-degree sextiles between Jupiter and inventive Uranus in late March, May, and November supply a plethora of fresh ideas that help us avoid repeating old mistakes. The pragmatism of Jupiter and Saturn in earth signs has a conservative side that would normally resist untested concepts. But Uranus's aspects with Jupiter weave intuition into the year's fabric to brighten it with originality. Jupiter's friendly relationships with the planets of the old tried and true (Saturn) and new and untested (Uranus) combines the best of the past and the future.

SATURN IN VIRGO

MANAGING THE DETAILS

September 2, 2007–October 29, 2009

Saturn, the planet of boundaries and limitations, takes twenty-nine years to orbit the Sun and pass through all twelve signs of the zodiac. It demands serious responsibility, shows the work needed to overcome obstacles, and teaches us how to build new structures in our lives. Saturn thrives on patience and commitment, rewarding well-planned and persistent effort but punishing sloppiness with delay, disappointment, and failure.

Saturn's passage through detail-oriented Virgo is a time to perfect skills, cut waste, and develop healthier habits. Saturn and Virgo are both pragmatic, which makes them an excellent pair for improving the quality of material life. Organizational upgrades and maintenance projects increase efficiency for individuals and organizations. Education and training become more valuable due to the increasing demand for highly specialized skills. Carelessness grows more costly, because minor errors can escalate into major problems. Systems break down easily, requiring closer attention than usual. Bodies can be more susceptible to illnesses caused by impure food or water, making this an ideal time to improve your diet. Environmental issues grow in importance as we approach a critical point in the relationship between humanity and planet Earth. Fortunately, Saturn in exacting Virgo is excellent for cleaning up unhealthy toxins produced by old technologies and in leading the way to develop new ecologically friendly systems for the future.

Saturn in Virgo highlights flaws and makes it easier to be critical of oneself and others. Yet its true purpose is to solve problems, not simply complain about them. Recognizing our weaknesses can sometimes be a source of despair, but the functional combination of Saturn's commitment and Virgo's analytical skills gives hope that effective change is well within our grasp. Small steps in a positive direction can slowly build up to a tidal wave of improvement wherever you place your attention this year.

MERCURY RETROGRADES

January 28–February 18 in Aquarius / May 26–June 19 in Gemini / September 23–October 15 in Libra

All true planets appear to move retrograde from time to time as a result of viewing them from the moving platform of Earth. The most significant retrograde periods are those of Mercury, the communication planet. Occurring three times a year for roughly three weeks at a time, these are periods when difficulties with details, travel, information flow, and technical matters are likely.

Although Mercury's retrograde phase has received a fair amount of bad press, it isn't necessarily a negative cycle. Because personal and commercial interactions are emphasized, you can actually accomplish more than usual, especially if you stay focused on what needs to be done rather than initiating new projects. But you may feel as if you're treading water—or worse yet, being carried backward in an undertow of unfinished business. Worry less about making progress than about the quality of your work. Pay extra attention to your communication exchanges. Avoiding misunderstandings is the ideal way to preemptively deal with unnecessary complications. Retrograde Mercury is best used to tie up loose ends as you review, redo, reconsider, and, in general, revisit the past.

This year, the three retrogrades are in intellectual air signs (Aquarius, Gemini, and Libra), which can be very useful for analysis and remedial studies that help you reevaluate what you already know so you can take your learning to the next step. Mercury has a natural affinity for the air signs, so you are empowered by your mental prowess during these times. But however intelligent you feel, don't become so enamored with the workings of your mind that you forget about the practical aspects of your body and the emotional needs of your heart.

ECLIPSES

Solar: February 6 and August 1
Lunar: February 20 and August 16

Solar and Lunar Eclipses are special New and Full Moons that indicate meaningful changes for individuals and groups. They are powerful markers of events whose influences can appear up to three months in advance and last up to six months afterward.

February 6, Solar Eclipse in Aquarius: Community Concerns
A revolutionary point of view can put an end to old fantasies and give birth to new dreams as mental Mercury and idealistic Neptune join the Sun and Moon during this eclipse. Aquarius allows a wide-spectrum view in which we can see our individual lives within the larger context of teams, groups, and community. Chiron, the Wounded Healer, also joins the eclipse point, which can increase compassion globally, give birth to new social organizations, and stir more interest in charitable activities. Charismatic leaders may emerge with fresh ideas for reinvigorating society. But it could be difficult to

determine which are capable of bringing about real change and which are simply masters of illusion.

February 20, Lunar Eclipse in Virgo: Fix What's Broken
This total eclipse of the Moon in critical Virgo reveals flaws in current systems, regardless of how much effort was put into building them. Serious Saturn conjunct the Moon reflects the hard work invested in the physical and emotional structures that are starting to fail now. A Lunar Eclipse is about letting go of the past, but both the Moon and Saturn are resistant to change. Virgo's analytical abilities permit us to justify these outmoded patterns with reason and practicality. But the Pisces Sun in opposition shows that the creative path of faith and imagination will take us farther than roads of duty, obligation, and habit. When daily details drain the joy out of life, it's clear that change is necessary. Yet we may feel the need to choose between a reality that's not fully satisfying and a dream that we fear will never come true. Fortunately, evolutionary Pluto forms a creative 120-degree trine with the eclipse that eliminates nonessential tasks to free up time and energy for more meaningful activities.

August 1, Solar Eclipse in Leo: Creativity Shines
Eclipses of the Sun are often associated with the fall of leaders. This one in the Sun's own sign of Leo is visible through central Russia and China, where changes at the top are most likely to occur. On a personal level, Solar

Eclipses are reminders to tame the ego and to balance will with humility. At its best, Leo is a sign of creative expression and generosity, but at its worst it represents a petulant, demanding child. Oppositions to this Sun-Moon conjunction from Neptune and Chiron add vulnerability and engender the kind of insecurity that may provoke immature behavior. Expect drama, but don't allow it to take over. Instead of giving in to the demands of others or to your own fears, step back and permit the storm to pass. This eclipse can bring healing through self-acceptance and recognition that even the biggest stories are only chapters in the book of life.

August 16, Lunar Eclipse in Aquarius: Make New Friends
This partial Lunar Eclipse is joined with nebulous Neptune, which could bring floods and fraud into the headlines. Otherwise honorable organizations may be touched by scandal or exposed as severely underfunded. Individually, this eclipse is excellent for letting go of beliefs that don't correspond with your current reality. Outdated ideals or dreams may need to be discarded, which can be painful, but awakening to today's truth brings a breath of fresh air that clears clutter from the mind. Cooperation is the key with Aquarius, so recognizing where friends and allies are more hindrance than help is important.

Remember that all of these astrological events are part of the general cosmic weather for the year, but will affect us each differently based upon our individual astrological signs.

2008
HOROSCOPE

LIBRA

SEPTEMBER 23–OCTOBER 22

OVERVIEW OF THE YEAR

Expect a tricky balancing act throughout the year between your innate need for relationship and the attention you must place on your inner development. Saturn, the planet of making it real, entered your 12th House of Spiritual Mystery on September 2, 2007, and will spend all of 2008 in this part of your chart. Your most precious accomplishments may not receive full recognition with Saturn in this behind-the-scenes house, but this can also give you a break from some of your worldly responsibilities. **Taking more time to tend to your inner life is a good way to gain strength, heal old wounds, and reassess your life purpose.** This is a period of preparation, Libra, when you're readying yourself for an enormous step forward, beginning with Saturn's entry into your sign on October 29, 2009. Still, you're far too sociable to cut people out of your life. In fact, even with the challenging changes, **you might be ready for a rebound when it comes to love.**

Two eclipses in your 5th House of Love and Creativity can shift the landscape in these vital areas of your life. The Solar Eclipse on February 6 is joined with inspirational Neptune to raise hopes of a more sublime emotional connection, and a harmonious trine to Mars may even provide a willing playmate. Neptune, unfortunately, tends more toward fantasy than reality, which could lead you astray in the pursuit of a more perfect union. The Lunar Eclipse on August 16 is also joined with magical but illusory Neptune, repeating the fantasy-chasing theme. It's certainly healthy to open your heart and mind to more fulfilling forms of love, yet if common sense is lost in the process, you could wind up with less than you expected. **The magic lies within you, so create through your own acts of art, style, and self-expression where you can direct the process and control the outcome.**

Expansive Jupiter in practical Capricorn implies that rewards must be earned by disciplined effort as you gain wisdom through your hard work. Last year, Jupiter formed two strategic trines with Saturn in fire signs that may have sparked a new vision for your future happiness. The planets of hope and reality form three more trines on January 21, September 8, and November 21, but this year they are in earth signs, validating your great ideas with a commitment to a concrete plan. Still, 2008 begins while initiating Mars is moving retrograde, so it's best to wait until it turns direct on January 30 to kick your activities into high gear. The "action planet" becomes even more influential when it's in your sign from August 19 through October 3. It's an excellent period to demonstrate your abilities as a creative self-starter. Working, living, or playing solo is not your idea of fun, but knowing that **you can be productive without the support and approval you normally enjoy can free you from having to compromise** your actions and accommodate yourself to the will of others.

NOTHING BUT THE BEST

You're a romantic, Libra, so even if disappointment in a relationship puts you on your guard for a while, it tends to drop again as soon as your heart begins to heal. The two eclipses in your 5th House of Romance this year, though, can signal a change of direction that's likely to impact you for years to come. If you've spent your life trying to make others happy without asking for much in return, it's time to stop. Vulnerable Neptune's proximity to the eclipses suggests that the cost of silence is too high and can leave you feeling disillusioned about love. Instead of always compromising, treat yourself as the precious person you are—one worthy of all the love you're willing to give and even more. You have a good chance to connect with someone new who inspires you or to bring a higher level of idealism into a current partnership, but what's most important now is how generous this person is to you. The secret to a successful love life is to expect the best for yourself and reject anyone who doesn't give it to you.

A SURPRISING TWIST

The seven-year transit of inventive Uranus through your 6th House of Work receives a boost from intelligent sextiles by visionary Jupiter on March 28, May 21, and November 13. These are periods when sudden opportunities arise to expand your professional horizons. You might get an unexpected promotion, a chance to shift to a more intriguing field, or a spark of inspiration that leads you in a totally new direction. There are real possibilities to break through boundaries that have been keeping you from finding satisfaction in your job. Learning different skills or acquiring specialized education, especially in areas where you never thought you could succeed, is key to a more exciting and rewarding employment.

BURIED TREASURE

Pluto, the ruler of your 2nd House of Resources, crosses the bottom of your chart this year, which can lead to a complete reassessment of financial matters. It could help you uncover lost or discarded assets, so scouring your basement, attic, or garage for hidden treasures might prove quite profitable. Income may be gained through real estate, especially if you can apply your good taste and creative abilities to increase the value of distressed properties. Your family is another possible source of material gain—either via inheritance or by your reclamation of a talent passed down by one of your ancestors.

LAUGHTER IS THE BEST MEDICINE

Variety is more than the spice of life: It could be your key to physical well-being in 2008. Unconventional Uranus in your 6th House of Health indicates a need for diversity to break up any rigid structures of routine that can sap your energy. Instead of sticking to one familiar diet or form of exercise, experimenting with several different ones can work to your benefit. Neptune, the ruler of your 6th House, is making a long-term transit of your 5th House of Play, reminding you that expressing yourself joyfully is a core element of reaching peak performance. Dance, sports, and adventures in the great outdoors are just some of the ways to combine fun with fitness.

FAMILY TIES

Optimistic Jupiter's passage through your 4th House of Home and Family makes this a great year for domestic growth. Spending time and energy to improve your living space is a worthwhile investment; the possibility of moving into a larger domicile also makes sense. However, this isn't about building a palace or paying for flashy furniture and decorations. A more utilitarian approach with a focus on quality and convenience will serve your needs more effectively. Jupiter, the Guru or Teacher, in this house can also turn your attention to family history. Whether it's research into your ancestral past or a reexamination of your childhood experiences, a growing understanding of where you came from will definitely help you get where you want to go.

THE ROAD PREVIOUSLY TRAVELED

Giant Jupiter, the long-distance travel and learning planet, is in your 4th House of Roots, which rewards you when you return to familiar places instead of seeking out exotic new ones. Trips that connect you with history, especially of your own family, can be enriching. It's best to stick close to home from the first of the year until January 30 while assertive Mars moves backward in your 9th House of Faraway Places, and again from May 26 until June 19 when Mercury is retrograde in this part of your chart. Educational pursuits are most worthwhile when they are well organized. A smattering of classes here and there or a course taken casually with a friend is probably not going to be entirely satisfying this year; rigorous programs geared toward developing specific skills will be a better fit.

PRACTICE MAKES PERFECT

With solid Saturn passing through your 12th House of Soul Consciousness, this a great year for serious spiritual work. The reality planet in earthy Virgo requires dedicated practice to develop this important part of your life. Patience and concentration will deeply enrich your inner life. Pay attention to details to align yourself with your higher purpose. Small steps taken on a journey of commitment can carry your spirit as far as you want to go. Study the works of masters whose lessons may be demanding—but will faithfully guide your inner development.

RICK & JEFF'S TIP FOR THE YEAR

Work for Your Dreams

Take yourself very seriously this year, for your aspirations are not merely hopes and your dreams are not just passing whims. They are seeds of your future to be planted in the earth, nourished by your conviction, and grown by your actions. You hold in your hands the power to take control of your destiny and change the shape of your future. There will be moments to play, of course, and times to fantasize. But respect those inspiring images by doing what you can to manifest them in the outer world rather than just allowing them to stay in your head.

JANUARY

YOU FIRST

Start the New Year with serious commitment, Libra, as the New Moon in Capricorn on **January 8** plants a seed of ambition in your 4th House of Security. Don't broadcast your big plans until you've done enough work to be certain they will take root. Action will feed your dreams, but too many words can dissipate its power. Patience is more than a virtue now; it's a necessity for reaching your goal. The Sun's entry into futuristic Aquarius on **January 20** illuminates your 5th House of Romance and Creativity and can lighten your mood with play and enrich your life with joyous spontaneity. Aquarius encourages originality, so experiment with new ways to express yourself personally and professionally. A fresh look or attitude will spice up your love life even if conservative friends don't appreciate your change of style.

On **January 21**, hopeful Jupiter and realistic Saturn make the third in a series of harmonious trines that began in **March 2007** and will finish on **November 21**. This is an excellent opportunity to assess your progress toward long-term goals, and make any necessary adjustments to get back on course. The bold Leo Full Moon on **January 22** in your 11th House of Groups can put you in a leadership position or provide you with a boost from a friend or colleague. However, don't let flattery charm you into taking on more than you can handle. Venus, your ruling planet, joins purging Pluto on **January 24**, which signals the need to focus on one or two core issues instead of scattering your attention across a variety of projects. Go-getter Mars turns direct in diverse Gemini on **January 30**, further tempting you to divide your energies, but it's best to avoid distractions now.

KEEP IN MIND THIS MONTH

Don't forget to tend your personal needs despite a growing ambition to make your creative mark on the world.

KEY DATES

★ **JANUARY 6–7**

speak up smartly

A tense square between sociable Venus in your 3rd House of Communication and stifling Saturn on **January 6** could make you feel put down or underappreciated. It's a good idea to express yourself honestly—but do this discreetly to avoid creating further conflict. Chatty Mercury enters your 5th House of Self-Expression on **January 7**, which helps you present your ideas in an intelligent and entertaining manner. However, Mercury's retrograde cycle in this house from **January 28 until February 18** may require you to do some backtracking in matters of the heart.

★ **JANUARY 12**

experimental emotions

Social plans may change suddenly with a challenging square between Venus and electric Uranus. Your likes and dislikes can rapidly switch, attracting you to unusual individuals or objects and turning you off to familiar ones.

Hair-trigger reactions can destabilize relationships and spur spending sprees. Exploring new tastes and desires, though, can be healthy as long as no one is hurt.

★ JANUARY 19–21

creative juice

Passions are powerful with a super-stimulating opposition between romantic Venus and impulsive Mars on **January 19**. Flirting and fighting are possible as interactions are intensified in both directions. Your usual well-mannered demeanor readily gives way to more extreme behavior. This force, though, can also be applied positively, making this a good time to utilize your artistic abilities instead of engaging in the complications of relationships. The Sun's entry into your 5th House of Love and Creativity on **January 20** adds confidence, helping you to carry yourself proudly, but your idealism and generosity make it easy for you to share the stage. Responsibility kicks in strongly on **January 21** with the Jupiter-Saturn trine, but don't let others' panic push you to overreact. Slow and steady gets the job done now.

SUPER NOVA DAY

★ **JANUARY 24**

down to the core

Sweet Venus joins dark Pluto on **January 24** before both march into demanding Capricorn. This conjunction can reveal underlying doubts about your self-worth and raise questions about control and power in relationships. It can be a descent to the depths of desire that evokes obsessive attractions—and yet it's also a chance to deepen your understanding of what you really want compared with what you're willing to give in return. This might not feel especially loving or generous, but a greater awareness of how you operate with others is worth the price. You are getting to the heart of the matter, the core of love, and questioning the quality of intimacy you have with others. Reevaluating your partnership patterns can be painful, but you can be repaid with a renewed appreciation for yourself that will bring more balance into all your relationships.

FEBRUARY

CHANGE FOR THE BETTER

This is a month of emotional extremes, making objectivity more important than ever. The fun starts on **February 1** when your planet, Venus, makes a conjunction with generous Jupiter and expands your horizons of delight. Their union in your 4th House of Home and Family suggests that entertaining at your place or spending to upgrade your environment is a wise investment. An Aquarius Solar Eclipse on **February 6** in your 5th House of Love and Play can fill you with hope, but nebulous Neptune's presence at this New Moon blurs the boundaries between fantasy and reality. You need to dream, Libra, and to allow your aspirations for love and harmony to grow. Yet if the delicate cord between the ideal and the real is broken, the disillusionment can be painful. Stretch yourself in the pursuit of greater happiness, but fill in the gap between where you are now and where you want to go with logic that helps you to complete the journey.

Sweet Venus enters your 5th House on **February 17**, casting you in a very attractive light. Your talents take center stage as you charm your audience. Mercury the Communicator turns direct on **February 18** to recover ideas and information that may have been misrouted during the past three weeks. A Lunar Eclipse on **February 20** is joined by karmic Saturn in your 12th House of Confinement, which can stir up old fears and unpleasant memories. If you encounter doubts, delays, and disappointments, dig deep—you will find the resources to overcome them. Regenerative Pluto's powerful trine to Saturn and the Virgo Full Moon indicates that emotional resurrection is close at hand, Libra. Disaster can be transformed into triumph.

KEEP IN MIND THIS MONTH

Moderate the mood swings of short-term highs and lows by keeping your eyes on the future, where the peaks and valleys will be mere bumps in the road.

KEY DATES

★ **FEBRUARY 1–2**

host with the most

The Venus-Jupiter conjunction on **February 1** brings out the party planner side of your personality. Your ability to manage complex events demonstrates your leadership skills while entertaining others and boosting your self-esteem. Retrograde Mercury slides past dreamy Neptune on **February 2**. It's an ideal union for imaginative fantasy—but a slippery combination when it comes to handling details and clear communication.

★ **FEBRUARY 6**

gifts from the past

Retrograde Mercury conjunct the Sun and Moon during today's eclipse deepens your thoughts and recovers long-forgotten creative ideas. Reflecting on the activities that have inspired you in the past can help you choose which ones you wish to pursue in your future. Vivacious Venus is sextile inventive Uranus as well, which helps you shake free of any unhealthy self-esteem issues that stand in the way of love. Unconventional forms of fun and an unusual new playmate can add sparkle to your social life.

★ **FEBRUARY 13–14**

hometown getaway

An awkward quincunx between Venus and Mars, the lovers, on **February 13** is not the perfect setup for Valentine's Day. Venus in Capricorn wants a fixed plan, while Mars in Gemini prefers the freedom to improvise. Try to stay flexible to avoid conflict. A lusty Sun-Mars trine on **February 14**, though, can save the day with high energy and enthusiasm. Make time for a little adventure, whether with a partner, a friend, or all by yourself. Foreign cultures can provide exotic experiences through food, movies, or music without you having to leave the country.

SUPER NOVA DAYS

★ **FEBRUARY 17–19**

lighten your load

Venus's entry into Aquarius on **February 17** frees you to express yourself with less restraint.

A more open attitude toward love and fashion encourages experimentation with less self-criticism and concern about the opinions of others. Mercury's shift to forward motion on **February 18** encourages frankness and progressive thinking. The Sun's entry into impressionable Pisces and your 6th House of Employment on **February 19**, though, increases your sensitivity on the job. Patterns that didn't faze you in the past can touch a nerve now. Rules are wearisome and bosses less tolerable. This is no time to ignore the physical and emotional toll of your daily routine. The Sun's helpful sextile with Pluto points out what habits need to go and the best ways to eliminate them.

★ **FEBRUARY 26**

heartfelt expression

Mental Mercury joins loving Venus, enabling you to see relationships with clarity and articulate your needs more artfully. Strong analytical skills and a broad perspective on your current situation make it easier for you to solve problems. Bright conversations please you and illuminate your clever wit.

MARCH

ADVANCE YOUR INTERESTS

This month's planetary dynamics demand more activity on your part, but it's definitely better to be led by your own ambitions than to tread water in someone else's pond. Independent Mars gets the ball rolling when it enters protective Cancer in your 10th House of Career on **March 4**, loading extra responsibilities at home and work onto your shoulders. The message, Libra, is not to just smile and cooperate, but to consider blazing your own trail, either personally or professionally. The Pisces New Moon on **March 7** falls in your 6th House of Work and Service, signaling a time to choose between exhaustion and inspiration. Rebellious Uranus is conjunct this New Moon, adding uncertainty on the job and, perhaps, stressing your nervous system. Before you invest more of yourself to hang on to the status quo, consider alternative ways you could apply your energy to free yourself from this pressure.

Your key planet Venus's entry into compassionate Pisces on **March 12** may tempt you to give ground to keep the peace, yet its purpose is to encourage you to be kinder to yourself and to balance work with pleasure. The Sun enters impulsive Aries and your 7th House of Partnerships early on **March 21** and opposes the Libra Full Moon later in the day. This Full Moon in your sign forms tense squares with potent Pluto and impatient Mars in a powerful Grand Square. It can bring relationship issues to a head and give you that last push you need to take your life in a new direction. If you're not ready for a major change, it's time to go into training to build up your mental, physical, and spiritual stamina in preparation for an ambitious move in the near future.

KEEP IN MIND THIS MONTH

Put your own health and safety first. No job is worth wearing yourself out, unless you are being driven by a higher purpose than profit.

KEY DATES

★ **MARCH 1**

relationship options

A testy semisquare between gracious Venus and controlling Pluto could back you into a corner. The excessive demands or withholding behavior of someone you normally trust can undermine your confidence in this person or cause you to question yourself. A deeper understanding of your own desires will help you decide whether to retreat or forge ahead.

★ **MARCH 6–7**

unpredictably brilliant

Venus joins boundless Neptune on **March 6**, spinning relationship dreams and fantasies. Your artistic vision may be sublime now, but a realistic view of love and money could be lacking. A stressful opposition between assertive Mars and dominating Pluto on **March 7** can load you up with work. Instead of treating all tasks equally, apply triage to the most vital ones. The New Moon's conjunction with eccentric Uranus on the same day can spike your life with chaos.

However, this New Moon sparks a super-smart sextile between inventive Uranus and strategic Jupiter—although not exact until late March—it fires your intuition with creativity.

★ **MARCH 13–15**

all over the map

A savvy Venus-Pluto sextile on **March 13** gives you a strong but subtle power of persuasion, while a highly productive Mars-Saturn sextile on **March 14** can vastly increase your efficiency. Mercury enters Pisces in your 6th House of Employment on the same day, blending the fruits of your imagination with your diplomatic skills. Venus semisquares jolly Jupiter early on **March 15**, spurring spending and romantic optimism, but an opposition from stern Saturn to your ruling planet later in the day jerks you back to reality and responsibility in relationships.

SUPER NOVA DAYS

★ **MARCH 20–21**

climb your own mountain

The Sun's entry into courageous Aries on **March 20** marks the Spring Equinox and opens a door to your 7th House of Relationships. But instead of jumping into a new project or taking the initiative in a partnership, carefully calculate your next move, as the Libra Full Moon on **March 21** is too powerful to be used naively. Your usual trust in others can backfire if your defenses are down. Macho Mars and militant Pluto square the Full Moon in your sign, requiring toughness and resiliency on your part. You can meet others halfway, but only after they've proven their trustworthiness and if it's in your best interest to compromise.

★ **MARCH 28**
influential charm
Venus joins Uranus as the two form a supportive sextile with Jupiter. You combine a sense of excitement with reliability that earns you admiration and attention. This is a good time to stretch your social boundaries and take risks in expressing yourself within a group or in a one-to-one relationship.

APRIL

TAKE IT TO THE EDGE

Relationships, your favorite theme, stay in the foreground this month as the life-giving Sun transits both your 7th House of Partnerships and your 8th House of Intimacy. The action heats up with verbal Mercury's entry into the 7th House on **April 2** to intensify communication with others. Sharp differences of opinion spark debates that can threaten harmony. It's vital that you speak up for yourself, rather than remaining silent to keep the peace. The New Moon in ardent Aries on **April 5** is also in your 7th House, planting seeds of new possibility in partnerships. Challenging squares from active Mars in defensive Cancer and expansive Jupiter in ambitious Capricorn expose conflicting needs between holding on to what you have and pushing ahead for something more. Loving Venus, your key planet, enters Aries and squares Pluto on **April 6**, which can drive romantic issues to extremes. Letting go of old expectations may be required to open the way to the next level of intimacy.

The Sun's entry into earthy Taurus and your 8th House of Shared Resources on **April 19** is normally stabilizing, but the passionate Scorpio Full Moon on **April 20** keeps emotions churning as you dig more deeply into the underpinnings of partnership. Reexamining your own needs, and the needs of the people you love, can begin to transform the nature of your connections. However, your awareness of a problem does not require its immediate resolution. Give yourself time to assimilate new insights and feelings about desire and intimacy before making any radical moves. Venus entering patient Taurus on **April 30** helps you ground your emotions and find the common sense needed to guide you in reassessing your relationships.

KEEP IN MIND THIS MONTH

The deep fear of loss or lack of love is not a bottomless pit where you will stay, but a turning point from which you can rise to greater heights.

KEY DATES

SUPER NOVA DAYS

★ **APRIL 5–7**

impulse control

The exciting Aries New Moon on **April 5** is packed with responsibilities, especially if you're playing the rescuer role. Assisting others is noble, but make sure they're working as hard as you. Spend energy advancing your own agenda—this can be a breakthrough time for connecting with the public or launching a new project. Venus firing into active Aries on **April 6** can trigger love at first sight. But whether you fall for a person or an irresistible object, karmically accountable Pluto's tough square to Venus indicates a need to evaluate your financial and emotional investments very carefully.

★ **APRIL 13–14**

keeping it real

With the squishy semisquare between Venus and idealistic Neptune on **April 13**, you'll feel like you're wearing rose-colored glasses—especially with a Mercury-Jupiter square that often leads to exaggeration. Stretching your mind and heart is fine at times, but a semi-square between sharp Mars and strict Saturn on **April 14** will quickly impose the limits of reality to end ill-conceived dreams. Come down to earth and focus on a task that requires your immediate attention.

★ **APRIL 19**

small bites

The Sun's entry into Taurus is rich with sensual potential. Indulging yourself with touch, taste, and sound soothes your soul and sweetens a relationship. But a crunchy sesquisquare between soft Venus and hard-nosed Saturn signals a need to control your appetite. Pleasure is best taken in small bites to avoid emotional indigestion or financial regret.

★ **APRIL 23–24**

too much is just right

Passion fires you up on **April 23** with a hot square between the lovers, Venus and Mars. Both attraction and anger can be dramatic, especially with enormous Jupiter opposing

Mars and squaring Venus on **April 24**. Excessive behavior may be unavoidable and too much fun to miss. This is a time to exceed the speed limit on the highway of love and the road to recreation. Choose the game you want to play and put all of yourself into it. You may not attain your goal, but you'll have a lot of fun trying.

★ **APRIL 30**

relationship review

Libra's ruling planet, Venus, enters your 8th House of Shared Resources, increasing your capacity to receive more love and approval from others. You may encounter individuals who lack generosity, however, and you might be tempted to accept whatever crumbs they offer. This is no time to underestimate yourself. You are worth at least as much as you give and should accept nothing less. Don't allow the stubbornness of someone else to stop you from speaking openly about your desires and, if necessary, renegotiating the terms of your relationship.

MAY

FINANCIAL FOCUS

The dependable Taurus New Moon on **May 5** in your 8th House of Deep Sharing puts you in a good bargaining position, thanks to a supportive trine from generous Jupiter. If you have a clear plan, your ability to gain the material and emotional support you need from others should be enhanced now. Some romantic magic is possible, too, what with blissful Neptune's conjunction with the Moon's North Node in your 5th House of Love. Serious Saturn goes direct on **May 2**, but expansive Jupiter turns retrograde on **May 9**, a complex combination requiring you to completely assimilate any gains before cautiously pushing ahead. Mental Mercury's appetite for information grows upon entering its airy home sign, Gemini, on **May 2**. However, its hard aspects to restraining Saturn and Pluto on **May 4** complicate data flow, a slowdown that will occur again when the Messenger turns retrograde on **May 26**. Keep in mind that you need to maneuver carefully to ride the waves of change when planets turn in different directions.

The Scorpio Full Moon on **May 19** in your 2nd House of Resources could bring financial issues to a boil. Yet nebulous Neptune's square to this Sun-Moon opposition may produce more fiction than fact. Careless spending, faulty calculations, and unrealistic dreams can be more costly than anticipated. Still, faith or forgiveness could get you through a tight spot, and inspiration may open your eyes to your own untapped talent. The second brilliant Jupiter-Uranus sextile of the year on **May 21** offers unconventional insights and flashes of intuition that can allow you to make a rapid course correction. The first two occurrences of this aspect may not be fully appreciated until the last one on **November 13**.

KEEP IN MIND THIS MONTH

Spending a modest amount of money on a small indulgence or two can satisfy your cravings without necessarily breaking the bank.

KEY DATES

★ **MAY 1–2**

recovered wealth

Venus forms constructive trines with no-nonsense Saturn and Pluto on **May 1**, creating a potent and practical Grand Earth Trine. Your sense of judgment about objects and people is excellent, especially when it comes to finding value that others overlook. You are able to increase the worth of material things with repairs or restoration and can even save a relationship that seems to have lost its way. Opportunities for learning or travel could open with mobile Mercury's entry into your 9th House of Higher Thought and Faraway Places on **May 2**. Focusing your attention on a single subject, though, may not be appealing, so don't sign up for any long-term courses unless you've been planning to do so for a long time.

★ **MAY 9–11**

choose your battles

On **May 9**, assertive Mars strides into bold Leo in your 11th House of Friends and Groups.

Your confidence, creativity, and courage could put you in a leadership position—or perhaps a pushy pal shoves you into the spotlight. Stay alert, for a Mars-Pluto quincunx on **May 11** can entangle you in a struggle with someone who doesn't fight fair. Be prepared to use all your force to prevail or, if you can't win or want to avoid conflict, cut your losses and back away.

SUPER NOVA DAYS

★ **MAY 18–20**

active sixth sense

Expect pleasant surprises on **May 18** when attractive Venus aligns favorably with optimistic Jupiter and inventive Uranus. Your innate understanding of human nature helps you turn an uncomfortable situation into a surprisingly enjoyable one. Trust your instincts, even if they lead you in an unconventional direction—you are blessed now with higher intelligence. A square between Venus and Neptune on **May 20**, though, is less reliable. Your logic might be blurred by misplaced faith or vulnerability. You may even be misled by someone who is strong on image but weak on substance. The Sun's entry into curious Gemini the same day tells you to ask questions and get the facts instead of making false assumptions.

★ **MAY 24–26**

earning respect

Sweet Venus's entry into fellow air sign Gemini on **May 24** usually signals a friendly and playful social environment, yet a testy quincunx from manipulative Pluto on **May 25** suggests that all is not as it seems. Confirmation comes on **May 26** when Saturn's square to Venus defines relationship problems more clearly. If you're feeling underappreciated, it's natural to be less confident and, perhaps, avoid confrontation. A simple, honest statement about your expectations, though painful, can be a powerful step toward regaining the respect you deserve.

JUNE

A CURIOUS TURN OF MIND

This month highlights journeys of the mind and body for you. Ideas are bubbling and your feet are itching as the chatty Gemini New Moon joins with Mercury and Venus on **June 3** in your 9th House of Travel and Higher Education. You are ready for fresh stimulation to overcome the predictability of your daily routine. Planning a voyage, signing up for a class, or connecting with foreign ideas and cultures can scratch that itch. Gemini's intellectually curious ruling planet, Mercury, is still retrograde, so the precise picture of where these urges might take you isn't likely to come into focus until the Messenger turns direct on **June 19**. Powerful Pluto backs out of Capricorn in your 4th House of Foundations on **June 13** to make one last visit to judicious Sagittarius. It will stir deep thoughts in your 3rd House of Data Collection before turning direct on **September 7** and passing back into your 4th House on **November 26**. Use this time to review major plans, especially those related to your home and family.

Pluto's presence at the Full Moon in Sagittarius on **June 18** adds a dark tone to a typically lighthearted lunation. This opposition of the Gemini Sun and the Sagittarius Moon illuminates your 3rd House of Learning and is rich with bright new ideas. But Pluto challenges your mind to dig more deeply and extract the meanings hidden behind hopeful words and playful conversations. Inventive Uranus is square this Sun-Moon opposition, adding an explosive element that prompts hair-trigger responses and unexpected events. Uranus, though, also brings brilliance in the form of lightning strikes of intuition that shatter your perceptions and open your mind to a totally new reality that could free you from the past.

KEEP IN MIND THIS MONTH

Give the world time to catch up to what your mind envisions now. A bold leap of awareness can take years to come down to earth.

KEY DATES

★ **JUNE 6–7**

smooth operator

A sweet sextile between Venus and Mars on **June 6** aligns desire and action to help you get what you want from others. Your will is strong, yet you have a delicate touch that helps you motivate people gracefully and with purpose. Groups bring out your creative skills, making you a valuable member of any team. Retrograde Mercury conjuncts the Sun and Venus on **June 7**, indicating an excellent time for reopening discussions involving unfinished business. You may change your mind about a previous agreement, but you're unlikely to alter your thinking again. Trust your perceptions: Right now you have a very clear sense of your needs and aspirations.

★ **JUNE 12–14**

winds of change

Anxious squares from Venus and the Sun to eccentric Uranus on **June 12** can upset your mood and your schedule. Uncertainty in relationships is possible, with rapid shifts of attitude that can take you far from your comfort zone. But these aspects also symbolize a desire for new kinds of people, objects, and activities. You are simply experimenting now, and no long-term commitments are necessary. Loving Venus forms a supportive trine with spiritual Neptune on **June 13** that helps you glue the pieces back together. A sense of wholeness increases trust and allows forgiveness. However, aggressive Mars joins the Moon's South Node in your 5th House of Romance on **June 14**, intensifying your emotions with powerful feelings of attraction or repulsion—and little else in between.

SUPER NOVA DAYS

★ JUNE 18–21

opposites attract

Venus opposes passionate Pluto and then enters watery Cancer on **June 18**, which is sure to push some emotional buttons. Avoid quick judgment: Your reactions may be too extreme. Mercury turns direct on **June 19**, and then the Sun follows Venus's path opposing Pluto and entering Cancer on **June 20**, the Summer Solstice. This intense planetary mix brings another wave of powerful feelings, along with the urge to make a profound change. There is a break in the emotional weather, though, on **June 21** as solid Saturn forms a stabilizing sextile with Venus. Additionally, an opposition between pushy Mars and passive Neptune describes the pursuit of a fantasy or an exhausting struggle that can be avoided with patience and common sense.

★ JUNE 25–26

slow and steady

A Venus-Neptune sesquisquare on **June 25** blurs judgment on personal matters, but is balanced by the strength of a Sun-Saturn sextile that adds stability to your professional life. Revolutionary Uranus turns retrograde on **June 26**, while the ill-fitting sesquisquare between visionary Jupiter and taciturn Saturn slows down any big plans. Don't let aggressive individuals provoke you into hasty action. An impulsive move now can cost you a great deal of time and frustration later.

JULY

GROWING AMBITION

Making your world safer is a key issue this month with the New Moon and Full Moon occurring in the security houses of your chart. The powerful Cancer New Moon on **July 2** is in your 10th House of Career, stimulating fresh ideas about your professional future. Attractive Venus conjunct the New Moon—and generous Jupiter opposite it—brings recognition of your talent and encourages your lofty aspirations. You're not ready to shift jobs right away, but seeds for change planted now can lead you to more rewarding work in the future. Mars, the planet of initiative, enters your 12th House of Privacy on **July 1**, making this a time to operate behind the scenes, tie up unfinished business, and develop the spiritual awareness needed to support your next big move.

Your ruling planet, lovely Venus, sashays into expressive Leo in your 11th House of Groups on **July 12**, which may raise your profile as a leader or key player on a team. This contrasts with Mars going into stealth mode earlier in the month and leaves you feeling pulled between the pleasure of being with others and the need for quiet time alone. The enterprising Capricorn Full Moon on **July 18** illuminates your 4th House of Roots, stirring an urge to take on new challenges. Memories of parental advice can prod you forward with their high expectations or hold you back with their doubts and fears. The needs of current family members could prove demanding, too. Ideally, this is when the New Moon's seed of ambition takes hold: You feel the desire for success growing inside you and commit to nourishing it with all your might.

KEEP IN MIND THIS MONTH

Fear and self-doubt are not signals to curtail your ambition, but points of focus to show where you need to apply more effort to get ahead.

KEY DATES

★ **JULY 3–4**

checks and balances

Relationships are complicated as socially sensitive Venus passes from an optimistic opposition with Jupiter on **July 3** to a restricting semisquare with Saturn on **July 4**. The first transit awakens a spirit of generosity that could leave you burdened with extra responsibilities. You may even overestimate someone or spend more than you should. The second transit brings contraction and accountability. You are likely to get a quick wake-up call if you go too far or expect too much.

SUPER NOVA DAYS

★ **JULY 9–10**

not much choice

A wide-open Sun-Jupiter opposition on **July 9** can fill you with hope and promises. It's appropriate to be optimistic, but remember that careful steps are required before you reach the top of the mountain. A sharp-edged conjunction between go-go Mars and stern Saturn on **July 10** leaves no room for slack, because you have very specific tasks that must be done now. Even if you can escape a tough job, there's more to be gained by finishing it off. Mental Mercury opposes purging Pluto and enters Cancer, repeating the message that completing what's already on your plate is essential before starting anything new.

★ **JULY 12**

return to self

You may feel emotionally squeezed early in the day when your planet Venus forms a complex quincunx with insatiable Pluto. This can represent a final showdown before you finally give up on meeting unreasonable demands and turn your attention back to fulfilling your own needs. Venus's passage into proud Leo follows, burning away self-doubt—with the joyful support of friends, who remind you of how wonderful you really are.

★ **JULY 22–23**

meeting as equals

Your public profile should rise during the next few weeks as the Sun follows Venus into expressive Leo and your 11th House of Groups on **July 22**, but the moody Moon in your 6th House of Work and Service can leave you feeling more like a servant than a star. This feeling will pass quickly when the Moon shifts into fiery Aries on **July 23** and you are ready and able to engage others on your own terms.

★ JULY 26–27
fearless leader

Intellectual Mercury enters creative Leo on **July 26** to fill your head with dramatic ideas that beg to be expressed. Fortunately, you have the tools to turn them into reality: A highly productive trine between Mars and Jupiter in practical earth signs shows you how to get the job done. Venus conjunct the karmic South Node on **July 27** may attract individuals with strong opinions who impress you with their self-confidence and charisma. However, trust your own instincts to guide you instead of following someone else's lead.

AUGUST

MAKING MAGIC

This high-powered month is charged up with two eclipses, two New Moons, and three planets entering peace-loving Libra. The New Moon in dramatic Leo on **August 1** is a Solar Eclipse in your 11th House of Groups that shakes things up with friends or colleagues. An overbearing individual can go too far, forcing you to take a stand. As hard as you try to compromise, the only way out may be to end the relationship. You may also need to reduce a grandiose project to a more manageable size in order to simplify your life. The unconventional Aquarius Full Moon Eclipse on **August 16** occurs in your 5th House of Romance, opening your heart to a profound experience. However, dreamy Neptune's conjunction with the Moon brings a dose of fantasy that can cloud your judgment. Put faith in your own creative abilities rather than in someone else's promises. There is a place for magic in your life now, but surprisingly it's something you can produce for yourself.

"Action planet" Mars raises your energy level when it enters your sign on **August 19**, urging you to be more assertive and to take the initiative with others. You know how to advance your interests with a friendly grace that gets you ahead without irritating anyone else. Mercury the Messenger enters fair-minded Libra on **August 28**, sharpening your thinking and enhancing your communication skills. Venus joins the party on **August 30**, where it highlights your beauty and charm through **September 24**. A small change in appearance can dramatically increase the favorable attention you receive and boost your confidence. The meticulous Virgo New Moon in your private 12th House on **August 30** aligns favorably with goal-oriented Jupiter and Saturn, providing you with the perspective you need to map out long-term happiness.

KEEP IN MIND THIS MONTH

When you like what you see in the mirror, others will as well. Trust your naturally good taste to determine the look that suits you best.

KEY DATES

★ **AUGUST 5–6**

stormy weather

Your confidence rises on **August 5** as Venus aligns with promising Jupiter and powerful Pluto. However, it's best to avoid overindulgence: On **August 6**, your ruling planet moves into refined Virgo, where excesses are not well tolerated. Explosive oppositions from Mars to fickle Uranus and from Mercury to fuzzy Neptune are far from calm. Miscommunications can trigger emotional outbursts, so make sure you have the facts before leaping into action.

SUPER NOVA DAYS

★ **AUGUST 13–17**

forces of change

A Venus-Saturn conjunction on **August 13** adds a serious tone to your day. Rewards or approval may not come easily; the message is to be specific about your desires and work hard to fulfill them. A soft Sun-Neptune opposition on **August 15** feeds your fantasies, but a strict conjunction between Mercury and Saturn demands critical thinking and concise communication. Sweetness returns on **August 16** with a generous trine between Venus and Jupiter that can provide deep satisfaction, even with the unsettling Full Moon Eclipse. A volcanic Mars-Pluto square on **August 17** stirs deep feelings about power and control. Directing this intensity with precision can give you the strength to resolve long-standing problems.

★ AUGUST 19

your turn

You are primed to plunge into action as Mars enters your sign to fill you with a surge of energy and a shot of passion. If you're passive now, you may find yourself in a defensive position or fighting someone else's battle. This is an excellent time to begin a personal project that doesn't require the support or approval of anyone else.

★ AUGUST 22–24

social inconsistency

The Sun moves into your 12th House of Secrets on **August 22**, which normally spurs a desire for less social interaction. But with artistic Venus opposite surprising Uranus on **August 23**, this is not a time to follow conventional patterns. You need the freedom to come and go as you please, rather than maintaining a constant presence with others. Nervous tension may build friction in relationships, but this can be overcome on **August 24** when forgiving Neptune aligns with Venus, allowing you to finally put the past behind you.

★ AUGUST 27–30
pushed to the edge

Conversations intensify as communicative Mercury squares domineering Pluto on **August 27**. Mercury moves into Libra on **August 28**, opening the way for more objective discussions. Then, on **August 29**, Venus repeats the pattern by squaring Pluto, pushing relationships to extremes. Your innate capacity to compromise is diminished as an "all or nothing" attitude prevails. This struggle can expose your deepest desires, which you can then manage in a more balanced way when Venus slips into reasonable Libra on **August 30**.

SEPTEMBER

WORKING IT

Work is a primary issue this month, but the good news is that opportunistic Jupiter in ambitious Capricorn turns direct in your 4th House of Roots on **September 7**. This can set off an inner process of expansion that encourages you to aim higher professionally. Investing in a home office or buying equipment to launch your own business is a smart move. Jupiter and Saturn, the planetary planners, form a constructive trine on **September 9** that effectively combines hope and pragmatism to help set a long-term strategy. This fourth contact in a series that began in March 2007 is a time to adjust your plans before a final commitment is made at the last trine on **November 21**.

Conditions are less stable during the sensitive Pisces Full Moon on **September 15**, which occurs in your 6th House of Daily Routines. The raw emotions, vulnerability, and vivid imagination of this event are jolted to a higher level of intensity by electric Uranus's conjunction with the Moon. You could be shocked by unexpected shifts on the job or in your health. However, this is also a time when a sudden flash of insight can free you from self-limiting ideas about your abilities and old habits that stand in the way of a more exciting professional life. A reevaluation of your assets is appropriate when Venus enters compulsive Scorpio and your 2nd House of Resources on **October 23**. Chatty Mercury turns retrograde the same day, beginning a three-week period in which you should review recent events, fill in missing details, and reconnect with people from your past. The New Moon in your sign on **September 29** provides a gentle push forward that encourages you to be more socially and physically engaged.

KEEP IN MIND THIS MONTH

Short-term crises can lead to long-term opportunities when you can let go of your unnecessary fears and visualize future opportunities.

KEY DATES

★ **SEPTEMBER 3–4**

eyes on the prize

The Sun slams into Saturn in your 12th House of Confinement on **September 3**, which can make you want to withdraw from the world. However, you can do some excellent work without other people to interrupt your concentration. The creative Sun's energizing trine to hopeful Jupiter on **September 4** gives you a picture of a more rewarding future. This is not mere fantasizing or escapism; it's a real source of insight about your potential. There are plenty of sources of distraction ahead, though, so don't overload yourself with peripheral activities that could keep you from your goals.

★ **SEPTEMBER 9–11**

personality plus

Pleasure prevails with a fun-loving square between Venus and Jupiter on **September 9**. You may toss good judgment out the window to play with friends or in a romantic pursuit of questionable nature. The desire to fill your heart can spur you to lose sight of your basic values and perhaps spend more than you should. It is appropriate to broaden your tastes and feed your senses, but keeping this within reasonable bounds right now can save you from regret later. A Venus-Mars conjunction on **September 11** continues the sensual theme. Whether you are seductive or shy, your ability to charm others wins friends and influences people.

★ SEPTEMBER 14–17
intermittent bliss

Talkative Mercury's conjunction with lovely Venus on **September 14** is great for sweet talk or discussing a difficult issue in a kind and thoughtful way. It can be hard to maintain your cool during the explosive Pisces Full Moon on **September 15**. If an edginess reveals your less-than-gracious side, take a break until you calm down enough to carry on a constructive conversation. Venus caroms off crazy Uranus with a quirky quincunx on **September 16** that can jolt self-confidence and rattle a relationship. Fortunately, a healing trine between Venus and spiritual Neptune on **September 17** shows a way back to common ground with others and wholeness within yourself, restoring peace and harmony in your world.

SUPER NOVA DAYS

★ **SEPTEMBER 20–23**

take your time

A tense Sun-Pluto square can undermine trust and provoke power struggles on **September 20**. Repressed emotions surging to the surface feel destructive, but can be a necessary step toward self-empowerment. A Mars-Neptune trine on **September 21** shows that you can be assertive and compassionate at the same time. The Autumn Equinox is marked by the Sun's entrance into your sign on **September 22**, helping you find your balance while a sextile between Venus and Pluto gives you access to deeper levels of intimacy. These aspects will serve you well when the love planet enters profound Scorpio on **September 23**. Its semi-square with strict Saturn and Mercury's retrograde turn, however, counsel patience above all.

OCTOBER

DOLLARS AND COMMON SENSE

Life becomes increasingly intense this month, driving you to earn more money and further develop your talents. Ardent Mars enters unyielding Scorpio and your 2nd House of Resources on **October 4**, prodding you to look more deeply into your financial matters. Reducing expenses to help pay off interest-heavy debts, for example, may require self-restraint now, but it will pay dividends later. The creative Sun's entry into Scorpio on **October 22** will shed more light on money issues and, perhaps, reveal underexploited abilities that you can develop to increase your sense of self-worth. The Full Moon in autonomous Aries on **October 14** opposes the Sun in accommodating Libra to put the issue of independence versus partnership on the table. Voluminous Jupiter square the Full Moon may push this polarity to extremes, leading to a showdown in which the choice appears to be giving in or going it alone. The real lesson is that successful partnerships require both a respect for the individual and a willingness to compromise from time to time.

Ideas and information flow freely when talkative Mercury turns direct in charming Libra on **October 15**. Venus, the relationship planet, wants more openness and honesty when moving into outspoken Sagittarius in your 3rd House of Communication on **October 18**. You are ready to speak more frankly about your desires and could even surprise yourself if you don't hold back. You need more than safety, security, and the same old boring routine. Love should make your heart beat faster now, rather than calm you down. The New Moon in relentless Scorpio on **October 28** intensifies your focus on increasing your cash flow. Carefully refining your budget and developing your assets over time can produce lasting changes.

KEEP IN MIND THIS MONTH

Tame your urges to act impulsively, but use the intent behind them to point you in the right direction so you can create a strategy to reach your goals.

KEY DATES

SUPER NOVA DAYS

★ **OCTOBER 4–6**

deal maker

Mars enters emotionally intense Scorpio on **October 4**, moving you past politeness to get to the bottom line. Tense semisquares between Mars and realistic Saturn and Venus and penetrating Pluto on **October 5** force you to protect your interests. Getting down to brass tacks involves tough-minded negotiations that may not show your generous side. Luckily, a hopeful Venus-Jupiter sextile the same day reveals additional options that allow you to take a stand without shutting the door on a possible win–win solution. Keep optimism in check, because squares from the Sun and Mercury to unrestrained Jupiter on **October 6** can make you too unselfish and undermine your recent gains.

★ **OCTOBER 10–11**

unique pleasures

A harmonious trine between joyful Venus and inventive Uranus on **October 10** can spark your social life with an unusual event, individual, or attitude. A Mars-Uranus aspect adds to your adventurous spirit, but could connect you with an unreliable person who has a sudden change of plans. A supersensitive square between Venus and Neptune on **October 11** is romantic and idealistic, but you could be easily fooled. If you decide to make yourself vulnerable to someone, Libra, first ensure that he or she is worthy of your trust.

★ OCTOBER 18

the great beyond

Venus shoots into heroic Sagittarius to widen your horizons of delight. A semisquare with "more is better" Jupiter adds rocket fuel to launch your hopes beyond the realm of reason. Going too far in the pursuit of pleasure or in your need to please others is almost too easy now. Avoid the temptation to have it all and do it all at once. You are glimpsing an amazing future; give yourself some time to reach it.

★ OCTOBER 24
power play

Passionate Mars in Scorpio forms a difficult semisquare with purging Pluto just two days after the Sun entered this emotionally complex sign. You may feel marginalized now and unsure how to fight back without losing your temper. Focusing on the specific issue, rather than an individual personality, will allow you to unleash your power with a precision that produces change without doing harm.

★ OCTOBER 26–27
in the lead

A square between little Mercury and giant Jupiter on **October 26** can turn a small difference of opinion into a major discussion. Exaggeration and miscalculation are possible, so stick to the basics to avoid becoming swamped in extraneous information. A highly energetic Mars-Jupiter sextile on **October 27** gives you the muscle and the motivation to be even more physically and socially involved. Your enthusiasm is showing in the best possible way. Wherever you go, others want to follow.

NOVEMBER

STRATEGIC PLANNING

You have the power to change the shape of your future with three major planetary aspects occurring this month. On **November 4**, conservative Saturn makes the first of five oppositions to radical Uranus in a series that finishes in **July 2010**. This stressful face-off connects your 12th House of Spirituality and your 6th House of Work, triggering upsets on the job due to boredom, lack of fulfillment, or an overbearing boss. While this can arise as a sudden crisis, it's not one you want to try to solve impulsively because your actions will have lasting consequences. A supportive sextile between optimistic Jupiter and Uranus on **November 13**, however, sparks insights that eventually might produce a more exciting career. The third major aspect, a trine between strategic Jupiter and Saturn on **November 21**, is the last in a series, giving you a new perspective that effectively combines optimism with reality to help you chart your course for the future.

Your ruling planet, Venus, enters responsible Capricorn and your 4th House of Roots on **November 12** to solidify your base with a sense of purpose and discipline. Yet a parade of planets moving into energetic Sagittarius in your 3rd House of Communication this month is bound to provide distractions. Active Mars arrives first on **November 16**, followed by the willful Sun on **November 21** and chatty Mercury on **November 23**. Your deeply rooted sense of fair play and desire for harmony may be challenged by a desire to assert yourself more strongly. Passion for your beliefs makes you an entertaining and persuasive speaker, writer, and teacher. A taste for debate can push conversations to the edge of combat, but with a playful attitude, you can have fun impressing others with your wit and wisdom.

KEEP IN MIND THIS MONTH

Speaking the truth can ruffle someone's feathers—but it's a price you should be willing to pay to claim your power.

KEY DATES

SUPER NOVA DAYS

★ **NOVEMBER 3–5**

emotional contradictions

Venus in Sagittarius forms tough squares to Saturn and Uranus on **November 3**. Saturn brings seriousness and restraint, and sometimes a lack of appreciation. Uranus, on the other hand, is a breakout planet that can provoke you to take social, romantic, or financial risks. You are feeling the pull between duty and freedom represented by the exact Saturn-Uranus opposition on **November 4**. It's best not to leap into action, however. A misleading Mars-Neptune square can waste your energy and leave you fighting phantoms. Calm your emotions and calculate your next move carefully—or simply take some time off to heal your spirit and gather strength. Mercury plunges into Scorpio to reveal secrets, uncover hidden resources, and intensify conversations. A sweet sextile between loving Venus and all-encompassing Neptune on **November 5** offers compassion and forgiveness, restoring your faith in relationships.

★ NOVEMBER 12–13

digging deep

Venus conjuncts profound Pluto early on **November 12** just before entering Capricorn to put a more serious spin on relationships. Unresolved issues stir deep feelings, even resentments, but facing them is healthier than denial. Respect is needed with Venus in ethical Capricorn, but it's something you have to give yourself before you can expect it from others. Venus in your 4th House of Home encourages you to make your environment more attractive and efficient. The Full Moon in sensual Taurus on **November 13** falls in your 8th House of Intimacy, increasing your desire to connect. Yet a square to the Sun-Moon opposition from nebulous Neptune blurs the line between fantasy and reality to create magic, confusion, or both.

★ NOVEMBER 16–17

clouds in your coffee

Mental Mercury's intelligent sextiles with Jupiter and Saturn add precision to your thinking and communication on **November 16**, even as active Mars's entry into adventurous

Sagittarius unleashes an urge to toss aside restraints and play. Imaginative Neptune is squared by Mercury and semisquared by Venus on **November 17**. Heightened sensitivity may enhance your creative powers, but fantasies can cloud your judgment and blur details.

★ NOVEMBER 27–29

jumping jack flash

The New Moon in Sagittarius on **November 27** emboldens you with fresh perceptions and strong opinions. Electric Uranus turns direct, bringing additional excitement. Facts can be fudged in the interest of making your case, which is fine as long as you won't be held accountable for minor errors. A clever sextile between Venus and Uranus on **November 28** rewards you with unexpected fun, while a Mercury-Mars conjunction increases the already rapid pace of communication. You get your feet back on the ground on **November 29** with a solidifying sextile between Venus and Saturn that clarifies your values and earns you trust.

DECEMBER

HOLIDAY CLEANUP

Powerful patterns during this month's Full and New Moons will spice up the season with intensity and potential conflict. The Full Moon in noisy Gemini on **December 12** generally kicks up conversations characterized by relatively benign differences of opinion. This one, though, is supercharged by a Grand Square involving five planets. The Sagittarius Sun is joined by aggressive Mars in your 3rd House of Communication, giving force to your ideas. Uncompromising Uranus and restrictive Saturn form tense squares to the Sun, Moon, and Mars that readily provoke arguments. The opposition between freedom-loving Uranus and law-enforcing Saturn intensifies this entire complex. You could experience brilliant breakthroughs of awareness; the challenge is in maintaining enough cool to keep discussions from boiling over. Fortunately, forgiving Neptune forms a creative trine to the Full Moon that can help you find common ground with those whose beliefs appear to be in direct opposition to your own.

The Sun's entry into traditional Capricorn on **December 21** marks the Winter Solstice as it crosses the bottom of your chart. You feel a deep sense of responsibility, but it's important to lighten your load before taking on any more obligations. A Sun-Pluto conjunction on **December 22** shows that it's time to let go of old expectations that don't support your current goals. The New Moon in Capricorn on **December 27** is conjunct tough guys Mars and Pluto, stirring up pugnaciousness in stark contrast with your normally peaceful and accommodating ways. Family members could simply be too demanding or push you too far. Don't repress your anger; focus it intently and you can channel its force to clear the air and finally put the past behind you.

KEEP IN MIND THIS MONTH

The price of peace may be giving up on your own convictions. Consider this high cost before seeking compromise.

KEY DATES

★ **DECEMBER 1**

inner strength

A conjunction between artistic Venus and exuberant Jupiter in your 4th House of Home and Family is ideal for beautifying your living space. Adding one special picture or decorative item can be enough to make a difference. Your confidence is running strong today as well, but it's the quiet kind that you feel inside and don't need to show off to anyone.

★ **DECEMBER 5–6**

war of words

Tension mounts on **December 5** with a Mercury-Uranus square tightening up your nervous system and a Sun-Mars conjunction placing you on a battlefield. You are in no mood to fight and would prefer to mind your own business and ignore the source of irritation. Still, this is your chance to kindly but firmly break news that you have been reluctant to share. Conscientious Saturn's square to Mercury on **December 6** demands that you face facts and speak honestly.

Fortunately, gentle Neptune's sextile with chatty Mercury enables you to express your truth with compassion, hopefully making it easier to hear.

SUPER NOVA DAYS

★ DECEMBER 11–13

fasten your seat belt

Quirky Uranus receives a semisquare from Venus on **December 11** and a hyperactive square from Mars on **December 12**—a pair of aspects bound to shake up relationships. Differences of taste and values are dramatized with the explosive Full Moon, when every desire for change encounters the limits of fear or habit. At the same time, mental Mercury enters strict Capricorn and immediately encounters penetrating Pluto, increasing worry and distrust. Give yourself time to absorb the situation rather than trying to sort things out immediately. A Venus-Saturn sesquisquare on **December 13** signals that self-trust must happen first and that patience is your ally in addressing these complex issues.

★ **DECEMBER 21–22**

descent to awareness

On **December 21**, the Sun enters ambitious Capricorn, a sign that seeks higher ground. But an intense Venus-Pluto semisquare can send your feelings plunging with disappointment or betrayal. The Sun then joins Pluto on **December 22** to take this emotional excavation to a deeper level. Be kind to yourself, but don't flinch when you see what's lurking in your depths. Even if the sight isn't pretty, getting to the bottom of your needs and desires clears up a murky situation and begins the process of recovery and transformation.

★ **DECEMBER 26–28**

hope springs eternal

An irritating Venus-Saturn quincunx on **December 26** may seem to hold satisfaction at bay. But active Mars enters efficient Capricorn on **December 27** to get you on a proactive track, while a romantic Venus-Neptune conjunction dissolves old disappointments in the refreshing waters of new hopes for love.

APPENDIXES

★

2008 MONTH-AT-A-GLANCE
ASTROCALENDAR

★

FAMOUS LIBRANS

★

LIBRA IN LOVE

TUESDAY 1

WEDNESDAY 2

THURSDAY 3

FRIDAY 4

SATURDAY 5

SUNDAY 6 ★ Speak up honestly, but discreetly now

MONDAY 7 ★

TUESDAY 8

WEDNESDAY 9

THURSDAY 10

FRIDAY 11

SATURDAY 12 ★ You are attracted to unusual objects and people

SUNDAY 13

MONDAY 14

TUESDAY 15

WEDNESDAY 16

THURSDAY 17

FRIDAY 18

SATURDAY 19 ★ Passions are powerful through the 21st

SUNDAY 20 ★

MONDAY 21 ★

TUESDAY 22

WEDNESDAY 23

THURSDAY 24 ★ **SUPER NOVA DAY** A journey to your core reveals your desires

FRIDAY 25

SATURDAY 26

SUNDAY 27

MONDAY 28

TUESDAY 29

WEDNESDAY 30

THURSDAY 31

FRIDAY 1 ★ Your ability to manage complex events makes you a great host

SATURDAY 2 ★

SUNDAY 3

MONDAY 4

TUESDAY 5

WEDNESDAY 6 ★ Inspiration is a gift from the past

THURSDAY 7

FRIDAY 8

SATURDAY 9

SUNDAY 10

MONDAY 11

TUESDAY 12

WEDNESDAY 13 ★ Make time for a little adventure now

THURSDAY 14 ★

FRIDAY 15

SATURDAY 16

SUNDAY 17 ★ **SUPER NOVA DAYS**
Lighten your load through the 19th

MONDAY 18 ★

TUESDAY 19 ★

WEDNESDAY 20

THURSDAY 21

FRIDAY 22

SATURDAY 23

SUNDAY 24

MONDAY 25

TUESDAY 26 ★ A heartfelt expression of your needs brings clarity

WEDNESDAY 27

THURSDAY 28

FRIDAY 29

SATURDAY 1 ★ Understand your desires to make relationship decisions

SUNDAY 2

MONDAY 3

TUESDAY 4

WEDNESDAY 5

THURSDAY 6 ★ Your artistic vision is unpredictably brilliant through the 7th

FRIDAY 7 ★

SATURDAY 8

SUNDAY 9

MONDAY 10

TUESDAY 11

WEDNESDAY 12

THURSDAY 13 ★ You're all over the map through the 15th—come back to reality

FRIDAY 14 ★

SATURDAY 15 ★

SUNDAY 16

MONDAY 17

TUESDAY 18

WEDNESDAY 19

THURSDAY 20 ★ **SUPER NOVA DAYS** Climb your own mountain

FRIDAY 21 ★

SATURDAY 22

SUNDAY 23

MONDAY 24

TUESDAY 25

WEDNESDAY 26

THURSDAY 27

FRIDAY 28 ★ Your charm is influential, so stretch social boundaries

SATURDAY 29

SUNDAY 30

MONDAY 31

APRIL 2008

TUESDAY 1

WEDNESDAY 2

THURSDAY 3

FRIDAY 4

SATURDAY 5 ★ **SUPER NOVA DAYS**
Control you impulses through the 7th

SUNDAY 6 ★

MONDAY 7 ★

TUESDAY 8

WEDNESDAY 9

THURSDAY 10

FRIDAY 11

SATURDAY 12

SUNDAY 13 ★ Come down to earth and focus on your tasks now

MONDAY 14 ★

TUESDAY 15

WEDNESDAY 16

THURSDAY 17

FRIDAY 18

SATURDAY 19 ★ Pleasure is best taken in small bites

SUNDAY 20

MONDAY 21

TUESDAY 22

WEDNESDAY 23 ★ Excessive behavior may be just right through the 24th

THURSDAY 24 ★

FRIDAY 25

SATURDAY 26

SUNDAY 27

MONDAY 28

TUESDAY 29

WEDNESDAY 30 ★ Speak openly about relationships and renegotiate if necessary

THURSDAY 1 ★ You find wealth that others overlook

FRIDAY 2 ★

SATURDAY 3

SUNDAY 4

MONDAY 5

TUESDAY 6

WEDNESDAY 7

THURSDAY 8

FRIDAY 9 ★ Choose your battles and cut your losses through the 11th

SATURDAY 10 ★

SUNDAY 11 ★

MONDAY 12

TUESDAY 13

WEDNESDAY 14

THURSDAY 15

FRIDAY 16

SATURDAY 17

SUNDAY 18 ★ **SUPER NOVA DAYS**
Follow your sixth sense through the 20th

MONDAY 19 ★

TUESDAY 20 ★

WEDNESDAY 21

THURSDAY 22

FRIDAY 23

SATURDAY 24 ★ Be simple and honest to earn respect through the 26th

SUNDAY 25 ★

MONDAY 26 ★

TUESDAY 27

WEDNESDAY 28

THURSDAY 29

FRIDAY 30

SATURDAY 31

SUNDAY 1

MONDAY 2

TUESDAY 3

WEDNESDAY 4

THURSDAY 5

FRIDAY 6 ★ Trust your perceptions; you're a smooth operator

SATURDAY 7

SUNDAY 8

MONDAY 9

TUESDAY 10

WEDNESDAY 11

THURSDAY 12 ★ The winds of change blow you from your comfort zone through the 14th

FRIDAY 13 ★

SATURDAY 14 ★

SUNDAY 15

MONDAY 16

TUESDAY 17

WEDNESDAY 18 ★ **SUPER NOVA DAYS** Opposites attract through the 21st

THURSDAY 19 ★

FRIDAY 20 ★

SATURDAY 21 ★

SUNDAY 22

MONDAY 23

TUESDAY 24

WEDNESDAY 25 ★ Slow and steady is the safe way to go through the 26th

THURSDAY 26 ★

FRIDAY 27

SATURDAY 28

SUNDAY 29

MONDAY 30

TUESDAY 1

WEDNESDAY 2

THURSDAY 3 ★ Seek balance between reality and expectations

FRIDAY 4 ★

SATURDAY 5

SUNDAY 6

MONDAY 7

TUESDAY 8

WEDNESDAY 9 ★ **SUPER NOVA DAYS** Be optimistic but careful through the 10th

THURSDAY 10 ★

FRIDAY 11

SATURDAY 12 ★ Turn your attention back to yourself and your needs

SUNDAY 13

MONDAY 14

TUESDAY 15

WEDNESDAY 16

THURSDAY 17

FRIDAY 18

SATURDAY 19

SUNDAY 20

MONDAY 21

TUESDAY 22 ★ Engage people on your own terms

WEDNESDAY 23 ★

THURSDAY 24

FRIDAY 25

SATURDAY 26 ★ You're a fearless leader, so trust your instincts through the 27th

SUNDAY 27 ★

MONDAY 28

TUESDAY 29

WEDNESDAY 30

THURSDAY 31

AUGUST 2008

FRIDAY 1	
SATURDAY 2	
SUNDAY 3	
MONDAY 4	
TUESDAY 5 ★	Miscommunications can trigger outbursts through the 6th
WEDNESDAY 6 ★	
THURSDAY 7	
FRIDAY 8	
SATURDAY 9	
SUNDAY 10	
MONDAY 11	
TUESDAY 12	
WEDNESDAY 13 ★	**SUPER NOVA DAYS** Change is in the air through the 17th
THURSDAY 14 ★	
FRIDAY 15 ★	
SATURDAY 16 ★	
SUNDAY 17 ★	
MONDAY 18	
TUESDAY 19 ★	Begin a personal project that doesn't need support or approval
WEDNESDAY 20	
THURSDAY 21	
FRIDAY 22 ★	Social inconsistency can build nervous tension through the 24th
SATURDAY 23 ★	
SUNDAY 24 ★	
MONDAY 25	
TUESDAY 26	
WEDNESDAY 27 ★	A struggle reveals your deepest desires through the 30th
THURSDAY 28 ★	
FRIDAY 29 ★	
SATURDAY 30 ★	
SUNDAY 31	

MONDAY 1

TUESDAY 2

WEDNESDAY 3 ★ Keep your eyes on the prize through the 4th

THURSDAY 4 ★

FRIDAY 5

SATURDAY 6

SUNDAY 7

MONDAY 8

TUESDAY 9 ★ Your personality can win friends through the 11th

WEDNESDAY 10 ★

THURSDAY 11 ★

FRIDAY 12

SATURDAY 13

SUNDAY 14 ★ Find the common ground to restore harmony through the 17th

MONDAY 15 ★

TUESDAY 16 ★

WEDNESDAY 17 ★

THURSDAY 18

FRIDAY 19

SATURDAY 20 ★ **SUPER NOVA DAYS**

Take steps toward self-empowerment through the 23rd

SUNDAY 21 ★

MONDAY 22 ★

TUESDAY 23 ★

WEDNESDAY 24

THURSDAY 25

FRIDAY 26

SATURDAY 27

SUNDAY 28

MONDAY 29

TUESDAY 30

WEDNESDAY 1

THURSDAY 2

FRIDAY 3

SATURDAY 4 ★ **SUPER NOVA DAYS** Protect your interests through the 6th

SUNDAY 5 ★

MONDAY 6 ★

TUESDAY 7

WEDNESDAY 8

THURSDAY 9

FRIDAY 10 ★ Unique situations spark your social life through the 11th

SATURDAY 11 ★

SUNDAY 12

MONDAY 13

TUESDAY 14

WEDNESDAY 15

THURSDAY 16

FRIDAY 17

SATURDAY 18 ★ You glimpse the great beyond; give yourself time to reach it

SUNDAY 19

MONDAY 20

TUESDAY 21

WEDNESDAY 22

THURSDAY 23

FRIDAY 24 ★ Make a power play for change

SATURDAY 25

SUNDAY 26 ★ You're in the lead and others follow you through the 27th

MONDAY 27 ★

TUESDAY 28

WEDNESDAY 29

THURSDAY 30

FRIDAY 31

SATURDAY 1

SUNDAY 2

MONDAY 3 ★ **SUPER NOVA DAYS**
Emotions contradict through the 5th

TUESDAY 4 ★

WEDNESDAY 5 ★

THURSDAY 6

FRIDAY 7

SATURDAY 8

SUNDAY 9

MONDAY 10

TUESDAY 11

WEDNESDAY 12 ★ Dig deep and face unresolved issues through the 13th

THURSDAY 13 ★

FRIDAY 14

SATURDAY 15

SUNDAY 16 ★ Fantasies can cloud your judgment through the 17th

MONDAY 17 ★

TUESDAY 18

WEDNESDAY 19

THURSDAY 20

FRIDAY 21

SATURDAY 22

SUNDAY 23

MONDAY 24

TUESDAY 25

WEDNESDAY 26

THURSDAY 27 ★ Fresh perceptions and strong opinions embolden you through the 29th

FRIDAY 28 ★

SATURDAY 29 ★

SUNDAY 30

MONDAY 1 ★ Enjoy your quiet inner strength

TUESDAY 2

WEDNESDAY 3

THURSDAY 4

FRIDAY 5 ★ A war of words lets you break tough news through the 6th

SATURDAY 6 ★

SUNDAY 7

MONDAY 8

TUESDAY 9

WEDNESDAY 10

THURSDAY 11 ★ **SUPER NOVA DAYS** Fasten your seatbelt through the 13th

FRIDAY 12 ★

SATURDAY 13 ★

SUNDAY 14

MONDAY 15

TUESDAY 16

WEDNESDAY 17

THURSDAY 18

FRIDAY 19

SATURDAY 20

SUNDAY 21 ★ Make a descent into emotional awareness through the 22nd

MONDAY 22 ★

TUESDAY 23

WEDNESDAY 24

THURSDAY 25

FRIDAY 26 ★ Old disappointment dissolves through the 28th

SATURDAY 27 ★

SUNDAY 28 ★

MONDAY 29

TUESDAY 30

WEDNESDAY 31

FAMOUS LIBRANS

Bruce Springsteen	★	9/23/1949
Ray Charles	★	9/23/1930
Linda McCartney	★	9/24/1941
F. Scott Fitzgerald	★	9/24/1896
Jim Henson	★	9/24/1936
Heather Locklear	★	9/25/1961
Barbara Walters	★	9/25/1929
William Faulkner	★	9/25/1897
Christopher Reeve	★	9/25/1952
Catherine Zeta-Jones	★	9/25/1969
Serena Williams	★	9/26/1981
T. S. Eliot	★	9/26/1888
George Gershwin	★	9/26/1898
Gwyneth Paltrow	★	9/28/1972
Ed Sullivan	★	9/28/1902
Brigitte Bardot	★	9/28/1934
Jerry Lee Lewis	★	9/29/1935
Miguel de Cervantes	★	9/29/1547
Bryant Gumbel	★	9/29/1948
Angie Dickinson	★	9/30/1931
Mark McGwire	★	10/1/1963
Jimmy Carter	★	10/1/1924
Walter Matthau	★	10/1/1920
Donna Karan	★	10/2/1948
Mahatma Gandhi	★	10/2/1869
Sting	★	10/2/1951
Stevie Ray Vaughan	★	10/3/1954
Gore Vidal	★	10/3/1925
Chubby Checker	★	10/3/1941
Buster Keaton	★	10/4/1895
Susan Sarandon	★	10/4/1946
Anne Rice	★	10/4/1941
Grant Hill	★	10/5/1972
Kate Winslet	★	10/5/1975
Mario Lemieux	★	10/5/1965

FAMOUS LIBRAS

Carole Lombard	★	10/6/1908
Yo-Yo Ma	★	10/7/1955
Vladimir Putin	★	10/7/1952
Simon Cowell	★	10/7/1959
Bishop Desmond Tutu	★	10/7/1931
Sigourney Weaver	★	10/8/1949
Jesse Jackson	★	10/8/1941
John Lennon	★	10/9/1940
Helen Hayes	★	10/10/1900
Brett Favre	★	10/10/1969
Thelonious Monk	★	10/10/1917
David Lee Roth	★	10/10/1954
Eleanor Roosevelt	★	10/11/1884
Elmore Leonard	★	10/11/1925
Hugh Jackman	★	10/12/1968
Luciano Pavarotti	★	10/12/1935
Margaret Thatcher	★	10/13/1925
Marie Osmond	★	10/13/1959
Paul Simon	★	10/13/1941
Ralph Lauren	★	10/14/1939
e. e. cummings	★	10/14/1894
Roger Moore	★	10/14/1927
Penny Marshall	★	10/15/1942
Mario Puzo	★	10/15/1920
Flea	★	10/16/1962
Oscar Wilde	★	10/16/1854
Angela Lansbury	★	10/16/1925
Eminem	★	10/17/1972
Rita Hayworth	★	10/17/1918
Wynton Marsalis	★	10/18/1961
Lee Harvey Oswald	★	10/18/1939
Evander Holyfield	★	10/19/1962
Viggo Mortensen	★	10/20/1958
Mickey Mantle	★	10/20/1931
Bela Lugosi	★	10/20/1882
Arthur Rimbaud	★	10/20/1854
Benjamin Netanyahu	★	10/21/1949
Catherine Deneuve	★	10/22/1943

LIBRA IN LOVE

LIBRA–ARIES (MARCH 21–APRIL 19)

You Librans are gracious and easily project your individuality through cooperation with other people. Your personality tends to attract people into your life who can become a mirror to you, helping you gain elusive self-awareness. You carry a strong sense of justice in all your actions as you uphold the equality in your relationships. Aries is your astrological opposite. Aries are less prone to join groups and have less need for harmony in relationships. They're rugged individuals who prefer to work alone, so you'll have to adjust to the extreme differences in character between you and your Aries lover. If, however, the Moon or Mars is in a fire sign in your chart, the differences won't seem so vast and your chances for compatibility are greatly improved. You will have to give your Aries partner a lot of latitude and enough room for independent action. Together, you'll need to find a middle ground that balances Aries' self-interests with your need for mutual sharing. This relationship can work, but don't expect it to be easy. It'll be like riding a see-saw as you go back and forth between your individual styles.

LIBRA–TAURUS (APRIL 20–MAY 20)

You will relish the down-to-earth joy of the Bull. Both of you love the beauty of nature, art, music, and design, but your Taurus lover might be more sensual than you. You tend toward an aesthetic and aloof personality coupled with a need for balance, especially in the area of relationships. You strive toward cooperation, whereas your bull-headed partner can find it difficult to compromise for the sake of peace. Their stubbornness can be quite frustrating to you, for you may feel that you're always the one who gives in. If, however, the Moon in your chart is in Taurus, Leo, Scorpio, or Aquarius, you can become a formidable opponent in negotiations with your immovable Taurus partner. He or she can offer you a practical approach to life that is simpler and more innocent than you have alone. Since both of you have Venus as your ruling planet, pleasure rules your roost—though it may be more mental for you and physical for Taurus. Ultimately, if the two of you have common values, you can be happy, for neither of you live outside the perimeters of your morals. This relationship requires individual adjustments, but you'll have many a romantic night dreaming about all the beautiful things you can do together.

LIBRA–GEMINI (MAY 21–JUNE 20)

You can merge with your Gemini into a happy couple—enjoying the beautiful and refined aspects of life. You may struggle to remain focused and grounded together, for as two air signs, you tend toward living in an idealistic world of ideas and dreams that can fail to produce results and practical success in the real world. If either of you have the Moon, Mercury, Venus or Mars in earth signs, you will be better equipped to deal with the day-to-day responsibilities of living. Without other planets in earth signs, yours is a mental relationship, so communication is of key importance to both of you. Your Gemini lover will stimulate your creativity, inspiring you to greater heights of expression. You, on the other hand, will help your clever Gemini to incorporate an artistic grace in what they say or write. Together, you are dreamers and schemers, and will love to delve into the infinite possibilities that lay before you. One romantic aspect of this union may include writing poems, letters, or e-mail to each another and creating lovely things of beauty to give each other as gifts. You may have found yourself a lifelong playmate, lover, and friend, and together you will keep each other young at heart.

LIBRA–CANCER (JUNE 21–JULY 22)

You have high ideals in your relationships and seek to understand your partner as a means to broaden your own self-reflection and identity. Therefore, you may assume a mental stance in a relationship, which is not problematic unless you're with a water sign, such as Cancer. Your Cancer lover is a deeply emotional and highly sensitive person who may be overwhelmed and even perplexed by your detached style. Your Crab prefers to feel their way through a situation, nourishing and protecting those they love with a giving and open heart. No question about it: you appreciate this devotion. On the other hand, you may feel burdened, even claustrophobic, by the ever-present and sometimes unspoken needs of your insecure Cancer lover, unless the Moon or Venus in your chart is in a water sign (Cancer, Scorpio, or Pisces). Your partner is addicted to the comfort that comes through sharing and commitment. In the meantime, you want to understand and think about a mutual union, yet in the end, your actual commitment and steadfast concentration may waver. Needless to say, this will irritate your mate. If you can work out this difference of character, you should be able to love each other with care and respect.

LIBRA–LEO (JULY 23–AUGUST 22)

You are normally not too judgmental, but with your refined sense of beauty you'll either adore Leos or find them totally exasperating. If you are already in a relationship with a Lion, you probably fell on the side of adoration. This is perfect, for your Leo mate needs outward displays of love and affection. Your Lion can bring new friends and social experiences to you, for Leo is generally optimistic and outgoing. And you do enjoy the social events and opportunities to meet new and interesting people. You do, however, have particular tastes that can, at times, seem picky—especially to your Leo partner, who is more concerned with fun and cheer than worrying about being in the wrong social circle. But as long as Leo receives a fair share of attention, things will remain at peace. One issue is that you can feel disdain for showy exploitation. This can be even more of a problem if your Venus is in Virgo or Scorpio. You'll have to open your thinking to allow your partner's friends to enter your life. You will be happier in this fun-loving relationship if you don't try to prune away your Leo's grandiose social life. Give your mate enough room to find amusement and he or she will open your heart in a way you never thought possible.

LIBRA–VIRGO (AUGUST 23–SEPT. 22)

You can have a difficult time making decisions because of your unique ability to see both sides of most situations. Accordingly, you make great mediators. But, unlike the other zodiac signs, you need a constant flow of input from others around you in order to know yourself or others fully. You move back and forth like a see-saw, from idea to idea, until you are externally motivated or forced to make a final decision. This trait will be difficult for Virgos, who are exact and finite about details and life agendas. In fact, you can make them quite crazy. You do enjoy each other's refined individual presentation and probably feel at home when you are around each other. In a daily routine, however, you will find yourself frustrated by your mate's impatience and criticism toward your changing mind. You two make good classmates and can help each other along a course of common study. As romantic partners, however, you're going to need help from compatible placements of your Moon, Venus, and Mars. Even with help from the romantic planets, you'll still need to make solid decisions and stick to agreed-upon commitments for this relationship to last.

LIBRA–LIBRA (SEPT. 23–OCT. 22)

Sometimes a relationship with someone of your own sign is a perfectly wonderful thing. You Librans, however, have an innate willingness to lose yourself in your partner. Put the two of you together, and you may flounder about, for without the presence of a grounding influence, this may be a pie-in-the-sky union without the means to bring it to fruition. Both of you are highly idealistic and artistic. Sure, you can build castles in the sky, but can you bring your relationship down to earth? When you're with another Libra, the placement of the other planets in each of your charts can determine whether you are mutually compatible. In particular, you will need good aspects between the Moon, Venus, and Mars. Regardless of these aspects, you can achieve great success with a Libra lover if you each practice sticking to commitments and making clear decisions that benefit the two of you as well as others. Together, you can enjoy creating music, art, poetry, and clothing, as well as writing love letters and sharing intimate thoughts. This can be a very sweet union, but again, the question arises—can you two stay centered enough to produce the stability needed for the long haul?

LIBRA–SCORPIO (OCT. 23-NOV. 21)

You adore elegant objects that represent fine taste and aesthetic beauty, and have the ability to transform your environment into a peaceful haven. Scorpio's resourceful and magnetic personality would just love to bask in the sheer elegance of your domain. Your Scorpio lover may enjoy indulging you with the physical pleasures and emotional passions of life while you adorn him or her with appreciation and adoration. The problem, however, is that you may find your Scorpio partner way more intense than you think anyone should ever need to be. You may be attracted by the Scorpio's charisma and want to understand the mysteries behind the veil, but as you look deeper, you may not like what you see. If your Moon is in a water sign (Cancer, Scorpio, or Pisces), you'll be better equipped to react to the powerful Scorpion's emotions, but if your Moon is in an air sign (Gemini, Libra, or Aquarius), you'd better run for the hills while you still can. You are happiest when everything in your environment is in harmony. Scorpio is happiest when passions are running high. If you're willing to take a journey into the shadowy realms of emotions, you just may find more beauty and magic than you can imagine.

LIBRA–SAGITTARIUS (NOV. 22–DEC. 21)

You enjoy outdoor activities where you can appreciate nature, such as environmental programs, community gardens, and hikes. Actually, you Librans make good city planners or designers who seek to bridge the harmony of the aesthetics of nature with urban life. All this bodes well for a relationship with visionary Sagittarius, who is eager to learn, travel, and trek afar for new opportunities. Your Archer will surely bring the bigger picture into your life, whether it's the need for adventure or the need to think about things in a philosophical or global manner. Together, you can blend your high ideals, crafted with the finer touches of intelligence and grace. One problem that may arise comes from your need for harmony and beauty, whereas your Sagittarius lover will forego such abstract pleasures for the next voyage. Unless your Moon or Mars is in a fire sign, you may not always be ready to pack a bag just because he or she has picked a destination. On a smaller scale, you could create little worlds of diverse possibilities right in your own backyard. With a bit of practical assertiveness on your part and an action plan between the two of you, a wide range of options is available for a progressive, harmonious life together.

LIBRA–CAPRICORN (DEC. 22–JAN. 19)

You're attracted to all things beautiful, and although your Capricorn lover may choose practicality over beauty, there is still common ground between you. Your relationship with a Capricorn can produce an environmental blend of your loveliness and his or her austerity. Your partner will be challenged by your "out-of-this-world" dreamy style, for the goal-oriented Goat is relentless about the need to focus on the responsibilities of daily life. It is not that you are lazy, Libra, but you are just not used to putting your nose to the grindstone like the disciplined Capricorn, and you may feel rather burdened by the harsh expectations of your partner. If, however, Venus is in Virgo or Scorpio in your chart, you might be more understanding of this practical way of living. You need time to dream of the fantasy world that you will build in the future. Your Capricorn partner needs to stick to the fundamental nuts and bolts, and needs to take care of business in the present. If the two of you choose to build your paradise on earth together, you'll need to buckle down to the daily routine of practical work while your mate opens his or her imagination to the importance of beauty in your lives.

LIBRA–AQUARIUS (JAN. 20–FEB. 18)

Because you seek harmony in all aspects of life, you're concerned with relationships in general and naturally take on the role of mediator. You find yourself a fine companion in eccentric Aquarius, who is also concerned with the intellectual quality of relationships. Yet there's a difference. Your Aquarius lover is less interested in romantic relationships than in the relationships between abstract ideas and humanity. Theirs is not a warm and fuzzy love, but a powerful idea that can create an unbreakable bond. Your Aquarius partner inspires originality in your aesthetic tastes, while you can help refine his or her radical opinions and blunt assertions. There's an inherent genius between you two air signs, creating a unique mixture of originality, grace, and intelligence. If you choose to have children together, your offspring may carry a wonderful blend of these potentials. Since both signs tend to be primarily mental rather than physical, the Moon, Mercury, or Mars in earth or fire signs in your charts would help you deal with the practical world. In any case, this is a wonderful pair where the two of you can find just the right balance between freedom and companionship.

LIBRA-PISCES (FEB. 19–MARCH 20)

You love to learn about life and yourself through the perception of the people around you. It's one reason why you're a relationship-oriented person. Yet there's an aloof quality about your approach to people that can dominate your personality if you become too absorbed in indulging your self-awareness. When in a relationship with a compassionate and universally minded Pisces, you may discover an avenue of selflessness that you've not previously explored. Pisces is not so interested in self-evolution as much as the continual evolution of the human race. On the surface this sounds like you have something in common, but more often than not, you two will need other indicators in your charts to create compatibility. If the Moon or Venus in your chart is in a water sign, then the emotional underpinning of your Fish won't seem so mysterious and difficult to understand. If the two of you are to prosper as a pair, you'll need to find an acceptable balance between working on achieving harmony in your own relationship and your humanistic concerns. Your innate grace and social skills, coupled with your lover's sensitive nature, can bring about a peaceful resolution to any dissonance you may meet along the path of your relationship.

RICK LEVINE When I first encountered astrology as a psychology undergraduate in the late 1960s, I became fascinated with the varieties of human experience. Even now, I love the one-on-one work of seeing clients and looking at their lives through the cosmic lens. But I also love history and utilize astrology to better understand the longer-term cycles of cultural change. My recent DVD, *Quantum Astrology*, explores some of these transpersonal interests. As a scientist, I'm always looking for patterns in order to improve my ability to predict the outcome of any experiment; as an artist, I'm entranced by the mystery of what we do not and cannot know. As an astrologer, I am privileged to live in an enchanted world that links the rational and magical, physical and spiritual—and yes—even science and art.

JEFF JAWER I'm a Taurus with a Scorpio Moon and Aries rising who lives in the Pacific Northwest with Danick, my double-Pisces wife, our two very well-behaved teenage Leo daughters, and two black Gemini cats (who are not so well-behaved). I have been a professional astrologer since 1973. I encountered astrology as my first marriage was ending. I was searching and needed to understand myself better. Astrology filled the bill. More than thirty years later, it remains the creative passion of my life as I continue to counsel, write, study, and share ideas with clients and colleagues around the world.

ACKNOWLEDGMENTS

Thanks to Paul O'Brien, our agent, our friend, and the creative genius behind Tarot.com; Gail Goldberg, the editor who always makes us sound better; Charles Nurnberg and Michael Fragnito at Sterling Publishing, for their tireless support for the project; Barbara Berger, our supervising editor, who has shepherded this book with Taurean persistence and Aquarian invention; Laura Jorstad, for her refinement of the text; and Sterling project editor Mary Hern and designer Rachel Maloney for their invaluable help. We thank Bob Wietrak and Jules Herbert at Barnes & Noble, and all of the helping hands at Sterling. Thanks for the art and ideas from Jessica Abel and the rest of the Tarot.com team. Thanks as well to 3+Co. for the original design and to Tara Gimmer for the cover photo.